WRITERS AND CRITICS

Chief Editor

A. NORMAN JEFFARES

Advisory Editors

DAVID DAICHES   C. P. SNOW

MORAVIA, as a novelist, short story writer, script-writer, dramatist, essayist and journalist, may be said to rank among the most genuine artists of our time. Stylistically rooted in the tradition of nineteenth-century narrative, his manner of telling a story is factual, cold, precise; his social and cultural awareness compelling. Yet, while his work has aroused much critical interest in Italy and elsewhere, in Britain the misconception persists that Moravia is interested mainly in exploiting the theme of sex. In this study Dr Giuliano Dego illustrates how, in a world where the social, religious, and moral beliefs inherited from the past are no longer acceptable, Moravia considers sex and money the only basic criteria for judging social and human reality. Taking into account the main trends of criticism and constantly working from a historical standpoint, Dr Dego provides a striking picture of the social and political background which influenced Moravia's books; and concludes that Moravia's main aim is depicting the malaise of the *bourgeoisie*.

Dr Giuliano Dego, himself a creative writer, has worked as a linguist in the Cybernetic Department, University of Milan, and as a translator and reader for the Feltrinelli Publishing Company. He has taught at the University of Glasgow and is now a lecturer in Italian at the University of Leeds. Besides making contributions to British and Italian newspapers and magazines, he has prepared the "Contemporary Italian Poets" section of the *Penguin Companions to Literature*.

MORAVIA

GIULIANO DEGO

OLIVER AND BOYD
EDINBURGH AND LONDON

OLIVER AND BOYD LTD
Tweeddale Court
Edinburgh 1

39A Welbeck Street
London W.1

First published 1966

Printed in Great Britain for Oliver and Boyd Ltd
by Robert Cunningham and Sons Ltd, Alva

CONTENTS

ACKNOWLEDGMENTS

For help in the preparation of this book I should like to express my gratitude to Dr D. M. White and my colleagues in the Italian Department of Leeds University; and especially thank my friends Raymond Hargreaves of the German Department, Leeds University, and Patrick Boyde of the Italian Department, Cambridge University, for the generous assistance they have given me in solving language problems.

Acknowledgments are due to Secker & Warburg Ltd., for the following works by Moravia: *The Time of Indifference*, *The Woman of Rome*, *Agostino*, *Roman Tales*, *A Ghost at Noon*, *Two Women*, and *The Empty Canvas*; also to *Fiera Letteraria* (Moravia, "Perché ho scritto *La Romana*" 3 Jul. 1947).

Other acknowledgments are due to Neri Pozza Editore (Limentani, *Alberto Moravia tra esistenza e realtà*); Giangiacomo Feltrinelli Editore (Del Buono, *Moravia*); Ugo Mursia Editore (Sanguineti, *Alberto Moravia*); Arnoldo Mondadori Editore (Debenedetti, " 'L'imbroglio' di Moravia)" in *Saggi Critici*); Casa Editrice Giuseppe Principato (Russo, "Alberto Moravia scrittore senza storia" in *I Narratori*); La Scuola Editrice (Scaramucci, *Romanzi del nostro tempo*); Sodalizio del Libro (Accrocca, *Ritratti su misura*); *Les Nouvelles Littéraires* (interview 17 Apr. 1947); Edizioni Morcelliana and *Humanitas* (Falconi, "I vent'anni di Moravia" 1950; Prini, "L'esperienza del 'negativo' nella narrativa contemporanea" 1957); *Mondo* (Gadda, "*Agostino* di Alberto Moravia" 3 Nov. 1945; Bocelli, "Moravia romano" 22 Sep. 1959); and *The Guardian* (interview by W. J. Weatherby 31 May 1962).

The photograph on the front cover is reproduced by permission of Gisèle Freund.

For
E. BOA

ABBREVIATED TITLES BY WHICH SOME OF MORAVIA'S WORKS ARE CITED IN THE REFERENCES

A.	=	*Agostino.*
B.H.	=	*Bitter Honeymoon and Other Stories.*
C.	=	*The Conformist.*
C.L.	=	*Conjugal Love.*
D.	=	*Disobedience.*
E.C.	=	*The Empty Canvas.*
G.N.	=	*A Ghost at Noon.*
R.T.	=	*Roman Tales.*
T.A.	=	*Two Adolescents.*
T.I.	=	*The Time of Indifference.*
T.W.	=	*Two Women.*
W.R.	=	*The Woman of Rome.*
A.M.	=	Alberto Moravia.

CHAPTER I

EARLY YEARS

When *The Time of Indifference* by Alberto Moravia was published in 1929, the critics realised that it was not easy to place this monotonous and disturbing novel, drawn with crude vitality, in the familiar context of Italian literature. It immediately assumed historical significance. Moravia himself remarked that "it was a great success—in fact it was one of the greatest successes in the whole of modern Italian literature. The greatest, actually; and I can say this with all modesty. There has never been anything like it. Certainly no book in the last fifty years has been greeted with such unanimous enthusiasm and excitement."[1]

Some of the articles in the Italian papers ran to five full columns. No mean success for a book, especially as the author, like most Italian authors at that time, had had to pay 5,000 lire for its publication. This sum, which was considerable in those days, was repaid when success was achieved, though Moravia never received one lira in royalties.

Since then Moravia has produced some twenty books: some bad, some good, some very good. His position as a writer has grown increasingly important, and his work has been translated into many languages. Some of his novels and short stories have been adapted for the stage and the screen. The film version of *Two Women* was a great success when it appeared in 1960-1.

Moravia's literary activities have always been very intense. He has been a script-writer, is now the film-critic of the weekly *L'Espresso*, and contributes short stories, articles, and essays to *Il Corriere della Sera* and other newspapers. He is also the co-editor, together with Alberto Carocci, of the magazine *Nuovi Argomenti*.

In course of time Moravia's problems as a novelist have naturally become more complicated: but for the critic there still remains the stimulus of finding in the works of his maturity the same tone and basic problems as in *The Time of Indifference*, though now broader in scope and more varied in implication: a world, or an underworld, call it what we will it is the world of the greater part of mankind; and in the twenty-year-old Moravia it had already found a faithful interpreter.

Alberto Moravia (his real name is Pincherle) was born in Rome on 28 Nov. 1907. His father, who was both an architect and a painter, came from Venice, his mother from Ancona. Though Moravia maintains virtually complete silence about his family, it is known that it was middle-class, and probably fairly wealthy, as the young writer's long journeys abroad would suggest.

Moravia tells us that, since he was a child, he took much pleasure in telling himself long and involved stories about imaginary characters:

Especially when away in the country, I would go off into the fields, or stretch myself out, my feet higher than my head, on a couch in a room of the summer villa, and talk to myself. I cannot remember the plots of these solitary narratives, I think they were adventures, dangerous episodes, violent and improbable incidents; I do remember very well however, that I took up the thread of the story every day at the precise point where I had left it the day before.[2]

These stories were, then, serialised novels of a kind: but they existed only in spoken form. Moravia seems to have kept this habit of telling stories aloud even when he began to write. *The Time of Indifference*, for example, was also written using this rather unorthodox method of speaking, or reciting the phrase out loud before committing it to paper.

In those years, and in the years to follow, Moravia, trusting to his subtle intuition, benefited directly from wide reading. In his father's library he found Goldoni, Molière, Shakespeare, and *Don Quixote* in translation; Ariosto, *Les Misérables*, a few works by Dumas and Zola, and, above all, Carducci.

Carducci was my author in those days. I knew something about D'Annunzio's political actions, but nothing of his works. At school I had a teacher who was a great admirer of Carducci, called Tambroni, who made me learn the whole of the *Ça ira* by heart. I became a republican and wrote many poems imitating Carducci's style: I can remember a very long one in 'classical' metre, which had as its theme the Battle of Piave. In the meantime, I went to school without achieving much.[3]

He went on writing verse until he was sixteen years old, when a tubercular infection of the bones, an illness which had plagued his childhood, forced him to abandon his regular studies.

This illness has been the most important fact of my life. The second most important fact was Fascism. I attribute considerable importance to the illness and to Fascism, since, because of them, I had to suffer much and did many things that I otherwise would not have done. It is what we are forced to do that forms our character, not what we do of our own free will.[4]

In all, Moravia spent five years in bed, the last two in a sanatorium high up in the mountains at Codeville, near Cortina d'Ampezzo. Here he joined the Viesseux library at Florence and every week received a parcel of books on all subjects, Italian, French, and English. All his time was given up to literature. On an average he read a novel every two days, in particular historical and modern novels, which led him to a viewpoint more European than that of any other author of his generation. He was methodical, and would read all of an author's works, even the minor and less interesting ones.

As I was reading because I wanted to, and not because I had to study, I was saved from that dislike of literature so often suffered by those who have attended school. The authors I preferred were those who most conformed to my taste, formed on modern and foreign writers: those, that is, who described dramatic and romantic situations with events, characters, and dialogues: Boccaccio, Manzoni, Goldoni, and Ariosto. These were my favourites. I received great pleasure in reading the plays of the Venetian—the perfection of the eighteenth-century dialogue gave me the impression of a metaphysical word-play. I took seriously even the most improbable situations in Ariosto and was delighted by his limpid style.[5]

To these we can add the names of Dostoevsky, Freud, and Joyce. Dostoevsky was to become young Moravia's master in narrative and dramatic technique. Joyce's influence is more subtle: it is to be sought in the use of the relationship between time and action.

Little by little, his interests expanded. He read the Spanish dramatists, Defoe, Stendhal and Balzac, Maupassant, and showed particular affection for the French eighteenth century, the century of reason, the enemy of verse and poetic contemplation. Here Moravia had already found a congenial habitat. Pirandello's influence later provided further corroboration of his early antiprovincial, antinationalistic, European outlook. Finally, we can add the names of the great comic writers: Petronius, Apuleius, Boccaccio again, Rabelais, etc., down to the Dickens of the *Pickwick Papers* and the Gogol of *Dead Souls*. By the end of his adolescence, Moravia was well read in French, English, Russian, and Italian literature.

At Codeville, his life was "the most monotonous and lonely life imaginable."[6] He was always alone in a room that opened on to a great balcony, the only witnesses of his solitude the doctor and the nurse. At nine o'clock in the morning his bed was pushed on to the terrace and he stayed there naked in the sun until sunset; then he was brought back into his room. It is significant that he made his motto "solo col sole"[7] (alone with the sun).

However, in that loneliness, and with all that time on his hands, Moravia had begun to write again. Excited by his reading of *Dead Souls*, he gave up the idea of writing poetry and started jotting down the beginnings of a novel which at the time did not yield appreciable results. He left the sanatorium in 1925 and was transferred to Bressanone. He still had an orthopaedic aid which he used for some years, and he walked with crutches. Too far behind now to pursue regular studies, he began to write seriously. *The Time of Indifference* was begun in the October of that year at Bressanone, far from any literary and intellectual environment, and continued during the next three years, partly at Bressanone and partly in Rome. While in Rome he met Corrado Alvaro, then secretary to the staff of the literary review '*900* edited by Massimo Bontempelli, and it was in the third number of this review that Moravia made his literary debut. His first short story, "Tired Courtesan," was, like everything else in that review, written in French.

Bontempelli had invited all the contributors to '*900* to write a novel. Moravia was the only one to submit a completed work in 1928. This was *The Time of Indifference*, but Bontempelli described the book as "a mist of words," and went on to say that the public demand was for adventure stories. A Fascist campaign for Salgari was at that time in full swing. Salgari, who had died in 1911, was little more than a fascinating writer of children's adventure stories: but in his books the Fascists had claimed that they could see an exhortation to battle and adventure: in brief, that "school of courage" which was thought appropriate for the "Fascist Youth Movement"; and publishers were naturally susceptible to the taste of the times. Moravia's manuscript was, however, accepted by the Alpes Publishing Company, with the bleak stipulation that the author should pay for the cost of printing: and the book came out the following year, July 1929. Meanwhile the young writer quickly began to contribute to various *avant-garde* newspapers and reviews.

REFERENCES

1. "Writers at Work," 1962, p. 189.
2. "Moravia allo specchio," *Omnibus*, 1937.
3. *Op. cit.*
4. Accrocca, *Ritratti su misura*, 1958.
5. "Moravia allo specchio," *op. cit.*
6. *Op. cit.*
7. *Op. cit.*

CHAPTER II

THE TIME OF INDIFFERENCE:
AN OPERATION OF UNMASKING

In 1929 nothing could have been more drab and depressing than the social and literary scene in Italy. Mussolini himself was the expression of his times. Brought to power in 1922 by the money of landowners and manufacturers, warmly fostered by priests and school teachers, highly praised by foreign countries as a great leader and a firm barrier against Bolshevism, he set out to change everything—by methods calculated to leave everything as it was.

As a young man, Moravia noticed nothing of this. He was not interested in politics, nor in criticising society, nor in revealing pessimistic ideas and sentiments. He read, he wrote, and that was enough for him. The problems he was trying to resolve were the problems of his own life. And yet, unknown to him, these were also the problems of his age. Behind his characters in *The Time of Indifference*, a corrupt and mildly perverted Rome can be felt complacently nurturing the then new régime.

Moravia was mainly concerned with a literary problem. He was trying to fuse the techniques of the novel with those of the theatre. This was no mean undertaking at a time when the *genre* he had chosen, the novel, was treated with contempt.

Fiction, compared to poetry, had never enjoyed much of a reputation in Italy. When Moravia published his first novel, the international reputation of Italian literature was still based on the names of its poets: Dante, Petrarch, Ariosto, Tasso, Leopardi. This can easily be

understood. Until the year 1860, Italy had been divided
and ruled by more or less benevolent elites, Italian
and foreign; for centuries literature had been produced
in and for the courts: and the courts were not interested
in problems. It is significant that Manzoni's *The Be-
trothed*, the first important novel written in Italian, did
not appear until as late as 1827, when the national
liberation movement was already taking shape.

If, in 1929, the Italian novel was going through a bad
time, it would be wrong to say that this was simply due
to the prevailing political climate. For centuries catholicism and political despotism had neither favoured the
dignity of the individual nor encouraged independent,
critical thought and observation. Italian writing had
been largely a game played by the *literati*. Style had
become the crux of all literary problems and this emphasis was exaggerated to the point where perfection of
style became the supreme achievement.

Attempts had, however, been made to reconcile narration and writing at a very high artistic level. But all the
time the second tendency was gaining more ground. Fiction does not need to divest itself of its poetic form in
order to become communication of experience. But to
obtain fiction that has relevance to life, the artist's vision
and interests and those of his public must first be recon-
ciled. This was not the case in Italy where for centuries
the poets, with few exceptions, had been gently lulling
the sensibility of the happy few in order not to break
their placid sleep.

It is no wonder, therefore, that when *The Time of Indifference* was published, it provoked a scandal. There
were protests and outcries from all directions. Many
critics, while hailing Moravia as a miracle of precocious-
ness, expressed their embarrassment and regret that such
a talent should be wasted on a "decadent" theme. The
book irritated many, and, because it was irritating, it
was on everyone's lips.

The story is a simple one, with a direct development of basic events. The family portrayed here has come down in the world, but does not accept the fact and still tries to maintain a glittering *bourgeois* facade in the face of approaching ruin. The tale, set in the Ludovisi quarter of Rome, consists of a dense and complete account, tightly and logically controlled, of the events of three days in the family's life. With a style stripped of frills and a natural steady flow of speech, the young author paints a canvas of customs and morals.

Carla, an ordinary bored girl, is the predestined prey of her mother's lover, Leo Merumeci, a shrewd business-man of forty-two. The crucial scene of love making is postponed throughout the first half of the book, and the resulting suspense acts as a catalyst. There are three other characters, each of whose characteristics are fully described, so that at times the effect is that of a stereotype comedy of manners. Mariagrazia, the mother, is a middle-aged widow. A nervy, emotional, whining egoist, her sole concern is to salvage the wreckage of a fifteen-year-old love affair in which her lover, for reasons of self-interest (he wants to get his hands on the family's villa), is still ensnared.

Mariagrazia's son, Michele, resembles Carla, in that he is weak-willed, absent-minded, and apathetic. He knows he ought to consider himself mortally offended in his role of "brother outraged by his mother's lover, in the matter of his sister's honour," etc. Instead, as the days go by, he becomes aware with growing terror that he is quite without those feelings which the terrible events happening around him ought to have inspired in him: the virtuous words and phrases which buzz around in his head seem ridiculous because they are simply empty words to him.

Lastly there is Lisa, Leo's former mistress. She is a plump, flabby, sentimental gossip who tries to become Michele's lover and so recapture something of her youth.

Michele rejects her, and, in a desperate attempt to prove to himself that he can react "normally" to the problems confronting him, he tries to avenge the honour of his family by shooting Leo: but he forgets to load the pistol. The novel ends with a glimpse of the future: Carla will force herself to marry Leo, and Michele will never achieve a satisfactory relationship with life.

Such is the bare outline of the book. But *The Time of Indifference* is not a novel that can be summed up so simply. Its basic features and its historical meaning can only be properly outlined in terms of the problems it involves, which are many and complex. Their limits were clearly defined by the Italian critic Scaramucci, when he noted that, since Mariagrazia and her family have no positive values:

A series of involved dramatic situations exists, in which characters move who are marked by a hyper-lucid intellectualism, who are incapable of any positive action, and yet are urged on by the torment of a necessity for choice which, nevertheless, cannot find support in any definite moral criterion, where the criterion of sincerity is rejected. In an atmosphere of perpetual conflict, of tragic solitude and of the insurmountable impossibility of communication, they are impelled by a feeling of insignificance heavy with torment. All their attempts at choice appear condemned at the outset to the most radical failure, so that no escape seems possible other than death or a passive acceptance which, from Moravia's standpoint, completes the requisite characteristics of negative realism.[1]

Here are Michele's words:

'All these people', he thought, 'know where they are going and what they want, they have a purpose in life and that's why they hurry and torment themselves, and are sad or happy. They have something to live for, whereas I . . . I have nothing, I have no purpose. If I don't walk, I sit: it makes no difference.'[2]

This is a kind of hallucinatory, extremely lucid mental consciousness. Michele sees himself living as though he were another person, his reflexion appearing in the mirror of his conscience, always present with himself in what might be called a state of paroxysmal schizophrenia. He knows quite well that he must act, break the encircling grip of his alienation from the world around him. Yet he does not succeed in shaking off his inertia, because such an action is suggested to him by a logic unrelated to his deepest instincts and moral sincerity. Filial love, hatred for his mother's and sister's lover, family affection—these feelings float on the surface of his spirit as on stagnant water, they do not reach down into the region of emotion. All actions and situations are alike:

. . . across the flat, blank screen of his indifference sorrows and joys passed like shadows, leaving no trace; and consequently—just as though his own lack of substance were communicated to his external world as well—everything around him was without weight and without value, fleeting as a play of light and shade. From these spectres which traditionally should have constituted the members of his family— his sister, his mother, the woman he loved, Lisa— other figures detached themselves according to circumstances and his own imagination, by a process of duplication that might continue *ad infinitum*. So that it was possible for him to see Carla as a girl of bad character, his mother as a stupid, ridiculous woman, Lisa as a shameless hussy; not to mention Leo, who changed completely from hour to hour as a result of other people's remarks and his own too objective impressions, with the result that, if for one

moment he thought he hated him, shortly afterwards
he loved him tenderly.[3]

He had to decide: either to continue being what he
was, that is indifferent, or else to accept a compromise,
and adapt his intolerable situation to traditional sys-
tems, with all that this would involve: the petty decep-
tions and meanness of everyday life, conformity in
actions and reactions, feelings of joy and grief which are
almost obligatory, like the ceremonial clothes worn at
weddings and funerals. Michele seeks, once and for all,
to shake off his inactivity by killing Leo: but the tragedy,
as has been seen, dissolves into farce. The initiative
passes to Leo, who does not hesitate to act decisively.

Fallacara[4] was the first critic to point out systematically
the uneasy refusal to face life and the sense of defeat
paraded by these characters so beset by indifference.
Above all he points out the atmosphere in which they
move: that of a tightly closed circle, of an inability to
express themselves. He argues that narrative literature
in recent times has been almost completely occupied by
the novel of inadequacy. With the aid of Freud and
Joyce the individual was no longer related to the world
but to himself. More than concentrating merely on the
will and on the forces of the soul in general, writers had
concentrated on the movements which determined these
forces. The more the individual was making himself
aware, the more apathetic he was becoming; the more
complex he appeared, the more insignificant he was
turning out to be.

Despite Fallacara's clear insight, it was another fifteen
years before a further Italian critic, Falconi, linked *The
Time of Indifference* and much of Moravia's subsequent
work with attitudes taken up by the existentialists. That
is, he revealed the clear pre-existence of an existentialist
Moravia, ten years before Sartre and Camus. Falconi
observed:

In *The Time of Indifference* there is a prior claim which has not been recognised, and which, it seems to me, we should no longer delay in bringing into the full relief which it deserves. *The Time of Indifference* is in fact a forerunner of the existentialist novel. In it the existentialism is instinctive, spontaneous, unsystematic, it only becomes thought out and elaborated in the subsequent work of the author; but it is not limited to what is generally termed the climate, the atmosphere of a work, but underlies the whole novel and lays the foundations for all the essential themes, so as to make it the first narrative work of its kind in any literature.[5]

Then, "to remove the impression of puzzling paradoxicality to which this observation might give rise,"[6] Falconi continues with a rapid comparison between *The Time of Indifference* and Sartre's *L'Age de la raison*, noting how, in both, not only are the same limits of time (forty-eight hours) rigorously observed, and the number of characters (five and six) reduced to a minimum, but in some way action and catastrophe repeat themselves, the catastrophe in the void. As for the characters, Merumeci and Delarue might be twins. Similarly Carla and Ivic.

The same kind of detailed comparison can be drawn between *The Time of Indifference* and Camus' *L'Etranger*. In both books there is a judicial trial, and a final catastrophe, though the chain of events leading to catastrophe is very different in each case. Then, both the protagonists are indifferent, incapable of achieving an open relationship with the world. Camus' Meursault however, is a silent and spiritless victim of circumstances, Moravia's Michele a bitter and suffering diagnostician of himself. But to insist on comparing what might be called external appearances is unnecessary. The feature common to *The Time of Indifference* and the works of the French existentialists is that the perspective, the fundamental attitude in which the characters are positioned, is not only diametrically opposed to the classical view of life, the ancient interpretation of "world-wonder," the feeling of admiration and curiosity at the appearance of life in all its "richness," "beauty," etc.; it is also substantially different from the view of all the great narrative writing of the nineteenth century, up to the period following the First World War. Even Proust and Joyce may still be considered the final and remarkable flowering at the extremity of the romantic parabola. They had certainly laid open new dimensions for man, but always in the traditional sense of assurance and values, inside the boundaries of a reality that was still controllable. Joyce's "stream of consciousness" is still an attempt to understand man.

In *The Time of Indifference*, on the other hand, there is a clear-cut sense of a reality which escapes us, yet is present as an eternal obstacle to every quest for comprehension, finality, and values. Later Moravia wrote in his "Frammento d'autobiografia":

The dominant theme of my work seems to be the relationship between man and reality. This may seem to some a strictly philosophical problem: in reality it is the fundamental problem of our time. It reached its most acute phase during and immediately after the First World War, as a result of the total destruction, through the war itself, of the traditional scale of values; a destruction which brought about the sudden disruption and the complete collapse of the relationship between man and reality which until then had been based on traditional ethics. Man found himself suddenly incapable of establishing any kind of relationship with the real world; the world became obscure and incomprehensible to him, or, worse still, it ceased to exist. *The Time of Indifference* and the other

novels which followed tried to express the urgency of
the crisis in realistic characters and situations. It is
precisely to this urgency that I owe my attention to
the sexual act, which is one of the most primitive
modes of relation with reality.[7]

Here is the root of the anguish we feel to-day in face
of what seems to be the indifference, or casualness, or
incomprehensibility of the world, and the absence of
any rational relationship between it and ourselves.
Titles such as _The Time of Indifference_, _L'Etranger_, _La
Nausée_, _Le Mur_ speak for themselves. The anguish, or
indifference, the split or "alienation" from the world of
objects is a sense of schism; it is the irritated, clearsighted uneasiness of Michele, and at the same time his
absolute incapacity for action: his failure every time he
tries (in a desperate attempt to escape from himself) to
come to a decision, to establish contact with other people
and life. The reason for this is not simply inertia on a
practical level, but inertia on an ethical level: hence
impotence in his affections and his love, inability to
communicate, a liberation of the instincts, and a hidden
fermentation of the idea of suicide. The one-way ticket,
hospital-asylum-cemetery, of which Pancrazi[8] spoke,
would not be wasted on Michele, and, up to a certain
point in her life, as we shall see, on Carla. After indicat-
ing a very strong hint of existentialism in the stifling
atmosphere, like that of a closed room, or, better of a
hospital room, which characterises _The Time of Indifference_,
Scaramucci summarises by saying that, in the same
perspective as Sartre's _Huis Clos_:

the whole novel and each of the characters seem to
move not along an open trajectory, or through the
meanderings of a labyrinth, but within an irremediably
closed circle, where nothing is possible except to turn
round and round eternally in the grip of an un-

changeable situation, of a static anguish offering no
possibility of solution or escape.[9]

But, at this point, we must correct the impression that
may have emerged from the critical writings we have
noted: it would be a serious error to understand Moravia's existentialism solely in psychological, metaphysical,
or "natural" terms ("human nature" motionless in
time), instead of, more concretely, in terms of "history."
Certainly the young Moravia was not conscious of the
way a man is shaped by history and his environment:

> I well remember that the important question for me,
> at the time of this first novel of mine, was that of
> fusing the techniques of the novel with those of the
> theatre; a question which is—as can be seen—com-
> pletely literary.[10]

And again:

> I did not even know at that time that Fascism ex-
> isted. . . . While I was writing *The Time of Indifference*,
> I was continually ill; I spent the greater part of my
> days in bed; my aims were purely literary.[11]

But again:

> At the beginning of my career as a writer I was unable
> to connect two arguments; I expressed myself only
> through images and dialogue, in short I had a very
> high capacity for representation, and almost none
> for reflexion. When I wrote *The Time of Indifference* I
> knew nothing of existentialism. The problems which
> my characters tried to resolve were, in the final
> analysis, the problems of my own life, and the fact
> that they were also, without my knowing it, the
> problems of the age, can be attributed to the faculty
> I then had of establishing a relationship with reality,
> without any concession to aesthetic or ideological
> influences.[12]

It is precisely here, in this faithfulness of vision, that one must look to find the historical meaning of *The Time of Indifference*: the book in which without any reflexion or elaborate critical consciousness on the part of the young writer, but through a completely instinctive, spontaneous, and unsystematic ability "to establish a relationship with reality," the urgency of a crisis is mirrored in realistic characters and situations. It is that complete collapse of a set of traditional values that allows an intellectual like Michele "to find himself suddenly unable to establish any kind of relationship with the real world"[13]; and for the world to become for him "obscure and incomprehensible,"[14] or else indifferent.

This is the mother speaking:

... She had never wished to know anything about poor people not even to know any of them by name, she had never wished to admit the existence of people whose work was laborious and whose lives were dreary. "Their lives are better than ours", she had always said; "we're more sensitive and more intelligent and therefore we suffer more than they do." And now, lo and behold! all of a sudden she was forced to mingle with them, to swell the throng of the poor and wretched. She was oppressed by the same sense of repugnance, of humiliation, of fear that she had once experienced when driving in a car that was very low on the ground, through a dirty, menacing crowd of strikers; she was terrified not so much by the discomforts and privations she would have to face, as by a burning sense of shame, by the thought of how the people of her acquaintance, all of them well off, respected and elegant, would treat her, of what they would say; she saw herself, in fact, poor, lonely, with these two children of hers, with no friends, since everyone would have deserted her, with no amusements, no dances, no lights, no entertainments, no parties, living in obscurity, in complete naked obscurity.[15]

One thing should not be overlooked: here, and in other similar places, however violently expressionistic the tone may be, we find not only the embryo of Moravia's future social preoccupation, but also the whole sense of the desolate limitations and the drab human state of Michele's class. And throughout the book the *bourgeois* world embodies this sense of squalor. "Perhaps one might think," Moravia then observes:

that in speaking of the *bourgeoisie* I am tilting at the windmills of an empty demagogic abstraction. But, when I speak of the *bourgeoisie* I mean my next-door neighbour, the people I see in drawing rooms, streets, bars, ministries. See how they dress, how they speak, how they decorate their homes, how they marry, how they die, how they love, how they take their holidays; and then tell me what right they have to turn up their noses at Sartre's books.[16]

A ruthless documentation, expressed in violent and expressionistic terms, which sometimes caricature, but are always made objective through the reality of facts. There is no inventive and imaginary dimension, only a real one. Sanguineti has observed that it would not be difficult to make an anthology of great sections of the novel, with a view to drawing up a new, up-to-date *Dictionnaire des idées reçues*, since *The Time of Indifference* is a kind of encyclopaedia of the fatuousness of average *bourgeois* conversation. A terrible topical repertoire is amassed in the dialogues, and a collection of the common places of modern *bourgeois* consciousness is to be found in the characters' unspoken monologues.[17] In Michele's eyes,

the whole horizon of *bourgeois* passions is revealed

without any possibility of mistake, as radically corrupt; the world appears to be populated with innumerable Leos, that is men who live in naked greed and cynical lust, having reduced the mechanism of their existence to the most rudimentary skeleton, to the simplest motives, to the only realities that, Moravia would say, it is genuinely impossible to reduce further: sex and money. . . .[18]

And now it becomes easy to understand Michele:

Everything here is becoming comic, artificial: there is no sincerity in it. I wasn't made for this sort of life.[19]

The circle tightens: against a human background which is static and incapable of recognising its own sickness, and is even complacent about this sickness (the "savoir vivre" of the *bourgeoisie*), Michele's is the first portrait in a gallery which will be filled as the author progresses—the gallery of Moravia's hopeless existentialist intellectuals. *Bourgeois* himself, that is shaped by his own class even down to the smallest details of his everyday existence, Michele succeeds, nevertheless, by the assiduous exercise of his intellect, in acquiring a consciousness (however vague it may be) of the foetid swamp in which he is moving. "In most of my novels," observes Moravia:

the hero is an intellectual. They are about middleclass people, and the hero is most of the time an intellectual because I am convinced that the only possible hero interested in the middle class is the intellectual—the kind who does not compromise with reality. Industrialists, doctors or tradesmen have to compromise with reality because their outside interests are more important to them than their own ideas. I have as my hero the man who gives most of himself to his own ideas, who does not compromise in terms of his own class.[20]

As the bearer of a desire for moral conscience and a sense of justice which he has very soon found to be useless to himself and others in the animal, organic, economic struggle which forms the basis of his society, his story will be, above all, one of the most bitter and ever enduring conflict.

> 'It's impossible to go on like this.' He felt like bursting into tears; the forest of life, tangled and impenetrable, surrounded him on every side; no light shone in the distance. 'Impossible'.[21]

And so at an earlier point Carla says:

> That's what I want to know, ... and how can we possibly go on like this, day after day, with this continual irritation, without ever changing or ever getting away from this miserable state of affairs, being satisfied with any stupid thing that comes into our heads, always arguing and quarrelling for the same reasons and never rising above ground-level, not even that much?[22]

But then the stories of the brother and sister diverge. For it is clear, at this point, that a choice imposes itself. When facing a world full of shameful egoism and impenetrable moral obtuseness, such as Carla and Michele face, a man either remains faithful to himself, as far as possible, and suffers in its entirety his own alienation (often the only form of moral dignity left to him, if he remains within his own class), or else he yields to external demands, and, so to speak, comes to be "absorbed" by his own class and becomes a convinced and operative part of it, accepting thereby all its laws, with their implications, since there is no possibility of half-measures. He will no longer be an "active principle" (a judging mind) within history. History will have degraded itself to "nature": outside the dialectic of life-thought, life-moral activity, but well within the limits of life seen as simple "existence," however amorphous, farcical, and (in the last resort, with iron consequentiality) dishonest such an existence may then be. As the saying goes, he will simply live and let live.

This is Carla's story. While the bitter conflict of Michele with his society is the story of his indifference, in the sense of a chronic inability to adapt himself to life, Carla's story is one of an adaptation which succeeds. But it is an adaptation which succeeds only through a form of grave moral acquiescence or compromise. This is a failure in the face of which Michele's inability to abandon himself confidently and degradingly to life almost takes on the shape of moral nobility. If the failure of Michele, a tormented and naturally static character (since he is held in the iron grip of a hostile reality), is on a strictly existential plane, Carla's failure is above all on a moral plane.

Carla's all-conquering need to escape (she has much less mental resilience than Michele has), naturally manifests itself in rather rudimentary terms, as a desperate attempt to change her everyday order of things —as she says over and over again, to begin a "new life" within her familiar world. She feels there must be a solution to her problems in the reality surrounding her. These problems are usually regarded as a transitory crisis, a crisis of adolescence, which is overcome as life gradually "matures" us and "gives us wisdom." The classical solution is marriage, for in marriage one leaves one order to enter another, and puts down new, firmer roots into society. And consequently, we have Leo, the man who knows "how to live":

> When you are doing one thing, you shouldn't think of something else. For instance, when I'm working I only think of working. When I'm eating, I only think of eating. And so on. Then everything goes right.[23]

In the last stages of *bourgeois* degradation, Leo is the

most genuine example, in *The Time of Indifference*, of a perfect integration with the surrounding world, himself almost a thing, an object of nature. Naturally Leo does not represent an ideal for Carla. But Leo is at one with society, he holds the reins; by force of history, he has the stature of a victor. And Carla abandons herself to him "so as to do something." Other ways out do not exist. And it is here, at the very point where her degradation begins imperceptibly to develop, that she thinks that she has found a way of being in rhythm with life. The die is cast, the circle closed. Now it appears to her:

'that Michele was ruining his own life.' And yet it's all so simple, she had thought, as she slipped into her Pierrot trousers in front of the mirror, and the proof of *that* is that, in spite of what has happened, I'm dressing up and going to the dance.[24]

But, observes Sanguineti, who has produced the most significant comments on alienation in Moravia's characters,

the final result of Carla's initiation, that deformed vulgar maturity that is shown in the concluding chapter, the maturity of a woman who is weary of examining herself and others, is no more than the passive recognition of the world's natural violence, the painful but extremely deliberate renunciation of every effort to resist.[25]

Life was what it was and it was better to accept it than to judge it; let them only leave her in peace.[26]

Carla's initial project is fulfilled. ('End it all' she thought, 'ruin everything'.)[27] Her ruin does not result, anyhow, from her seduction: it results from her marriage. Carla, it is clear, will become like her mother.

The Time of Indifference shows the direction in which

the greater part of Moravia's subsequent production was to move; it illustrates above all an interest of a psychological kind in the "characters." Within this "psychological" dimension, however, a social interest is already taking shape in a rudimentary and instinctive way, finding expression in two particular forms of the relationship between individual and reality: that of the honest *bourgeois* intellectual ("who gives most of himself to his own ideas"[28]) and that of the ordinary *bourgeois*, who must constantly come to a compromise with reality. Moravia appears above all to be occupied with the daily relentless struggle for life, with the lack of sincerity and love among men, and with their anguish in the absence of all ideals. *Bourgeois* society has evolved in such a way that all this is inevitable. It is not that a new, different notion of reality is "created." It imposes itself. Moravia's great merit was to realise in time not only that things had changed, but also that the relationship between men and things had changed. It was the challenging and dangerous new note introduced by *The Time of Indifference*, the courage of indifference and doubt. Face-to-face with all the immoral attitudes fatally implicit in a certain social order, and with all the suicidal attempts at morality (the resumption of nationalistic and "moralistic" attitudes in the inter-war years, demolished by the reality of the concentration camps and Hiroshima) there stands the indifferent Michele. A lucid diagnostician of himself, the first existentialist character disarms himself by means of knowledge.

Except that Michele does not go far enough; or, if you like, he goes too far. One constantly experiences in *The Time of Indifference* the feeling of a radical refusal. Existentialism, freeing man from a long series of false superstructures and offering a more lucid notion of human slavery, has been in western literature the great cleansing operation of the century and contains a possibility of rebuilding and renewal. Moravia, on the

other hand, seems to enclose this world in negation
with an excessive, stifling fatalism, suggesting no way
of escape. Though a form of moral dignity is admitted
in simple withdrawal, Michele's withdrawal at times
becomes no more than a sort of complacent, total negation of reality—of all reality. No landscape, no book,
no hope can stir Michele. And Michele ends up by
being more than an alienated character, by assuming
the form of a symbol, an abstract outline of alienation,
so that, at certain moments, he even gives the feeling
not only of a crisis of a historical kind, but also of a
strictly personal apathy, of a pathological insufficiency.
"It is true" observes Moravia:

the character of Michele is negative in its results, yet
it represents the greatest effort I was able to make in
the conditions in which I was living at that time.
There always exists for an artist a resistance in reality,
a limit he cannot manage to overcome, an opaqueness
he cannot pierce; just as on a foggy night car head-
lamps cannot light the way more than a certain
distance. And then I was very young and I was living
the problem on the inside, I could not find my way out,
and it is already a considerable achievement that I
constructed this character and felt his despair without
understanding it. I did not bring him to any solution,
for the simple reason that I did not possess sufficient
energy, the resistance of reality brought me to a halt.[29]

Scepticism, despair, escapism, panic in the face of
reality, are constantly carried in Michele to the level of
hysteria. Nevertheless Michele is the first existentialist
character in the literature of Europe, and as such he
carries in him, exaggerated to the level of instinct, as
in the extremism of all discoveries, all those ferments
which are to give rise to the enquiry into the negative in
contemporary literature. Here, as Prini puts it,

ambiguity exists in the uncontrolled assumption of the negative, with no possible way of dividing that part of it which is linked with our natural existence as creators, from that part which is the result of a transgression or rejection of our limits. Hence we are brought to recognise the fact that novel writing, by putting itself forward as an experimental enquiry into the negative, has never required of the artist as lucid and as unshakeable a moral conscience as it has now. The experimental enquiry into the negative holds terrible dangers, since looking into the abyss can bring on vertigo, and then a fall. Unflinching muscles and clear eyesight are necessary. One must sense the vertigo of non-existence in order to arrive at a new, sincere and vehement affirmation of existence.[30]

The Moravia of *The Time of Indifference*, a twenty-year-old writer, did not see this danger. But once or twice the shadow of a dream, a nostalgia for something he has never had and which already seems lost forever, is there, in Michele:

His loneliness, his conversations with Lisa, had made him conscious of a great need for companionship and love, an intense hope that he might find, amongst all the people in the world, some woman whom he could love sincerely, without irony and without resignation. 'A true woman,' he thought 'a pure woman, neither false nor stupid nor corrupt. If I could only find her, it would straighten everything out.' At the moment he was failing to find her, indeed he did not even know where to look for her; but he had her image in his mind, half ideal and half material, mingling confusedly with the other figures of that fantastic world, that world governed by instinct and sincerity in which he longed to live.[31]

This, with larger implications, is later to be the

M C

"all-consuming-dream" of "the land of innocence" of
Agostino and of so many characters who are yet to
come: their awareness of some possible dignity, their
moral dignity.

REFERENCES

1. Scaramucci, "Moravia tra esistenzialismo e freudismo," 1956, pp. 87-130.
2. *T.I.*, p. 123.
3. *T.I.*, pp. 248-9.
4. Fallacara, in *Frontespizio*, 1935.
5. Falconi, "I vent'anni di Moravia," 1950, pp. 189-205.
6. *Op. cit.*
7. Limentani, *A.M. tra esistenza e realtà*, 1962, p. 95.
8. Pancrazi, "Il realismo di Moravia," 1946, pp. 118-22.
9. Scaramucci, *op. cit.*
10. *Confessioni di scrittori*, 1951.
11. *L'Espresso*, 2 Aug. 1959, p. 11.
12. Del Buono, *Moravia*, 1962, p. 20.
13. Limentani, *op. cit.*, p. 25.
14. *Op. cit.*, p. 95.
15. *T.I.*, p. 23.
16. Moravia, "Dopoguerra bigotto," 1947.
17. Sanguineti, *Alberto Moravia*, 1962, p. 20.
18. *Op. cit.*, p. 41.
19. *T.I.*, p. 153.
20. *The Guardian*, 31 May 1962.
21. *T.I.*, p. 314.
22. *T.I.*, p. 73.
23. *T.I.*, p. 16.
24. *T.I.*, p. 314.
25. Sanguineti, *op. cit.*, p. 20.
26. *T.I.*, p. 308.
27. *T.I.*, p. 8.
28. *The Guardian*, 31 May 1962.
29. Del Buono, *op. cit.*, p. 29.
30. Prini, "L'esperienza del 'negativo' nella narrativa contemporanea," 1957, pp. 527-36.
31. *T.I.*, p. 150.

CHAPTER III

SHORT STORIES, JOURNEYS, SECOND NOVEL

After his first novel, Moravia's art immediately shows an insistence upon those themes of sex, alienation, and moral vice which are going to be the basic themes of all his work. In the novels and stories which he wrote between *The Time of Indifference* and *Roman Tales* and *Two Women* (both of which have a social slant) Moravia's art shows itself more and more clearly, illuminating as through a prism one facet after another of the social world which we have as yet barely glimpsed. The eye of the novelist must have fidelity of vision, and will not admit obstacles. Behind such a quest, there is still the stubbornness of someone who, more than for specific moral reasons, or as a protestation against social injustice, wishes to vent his personal rancour against the limits of life. One of his vital needs is that of exposing the apparatus of lies beneath the hypocrisies, the false appearances. Moravia does not accept that one thing may pass itself off as another. Precisely because he is too violently involved and too accusatory (as we have seen in his portrayal of Michele) he sometimes ends by distorting and impoverishing his characters, through submitting them to too fierce a diagnosis.

Eleven short stories, collected together under the title *La Bella Vita* (*The Happy Life*) came out in February 1935. The French version of "Tired Courtesan" had already appeared, two years before *The Time of Indifference*, in the third number of Bontempelli's review, '*900*. It is the story of a young man who one fine day decides to get

rid of his ageing mistress. Having spent an entire afternoon torn by worry and doubt, he finally acts, and slips
from her bed late at night to go to the cinema. The story
has all the obvious faults of a literary novice: rhetoric,
facile effects, melodrama, etc. Beside the forced surrealistic tones ("The room was a cube of white light
with the two lovers inside like two well-preserved
corpses in a block of mortuary ice"), there are clear
echoes of D'Annunzio, and an almost jaunty air. At
times the tale becomes forced and uncertain; and yet
it remains, especially in the descriptive passages, the first
indication of a writer of quality. Here, two years before
The Time of Indifference, Moravia had already found the
language most appropriate and the standpoint most
suited to his temperament as a novelist. Moreover
psychological conflict and the ragings of the flesh are
going to be the essence of Moravia's future intellectual
bourgeois: a man of persistent and subtle intelligence,
with a completely worldly outlook, always foiled in his
search for a way out of his anguish.

One of the stories of this collection, "A Sick Boy's
Winter," written in 1930, is justly famous. Here too
Moravia keeps very strictly to the naturalism of events.
He will not accept abstractions. But, apart from details
of the plot, the new and more important feature of this
story is the reticent and compassionate way in which he
tells it. His main attack is directed, as always, against
the *bourgeoisie*, which he blames for hypocritically shelter-
ing the boy Gerolamo: but he also shows a touching
understanding for Gerolamo himself, as the boy is
suddenly brought into contact with the painful reality
of life. Moravia is not Gerolamo, just as he is not
Tancredi of "The Fall," Agostino, Luca of *Disobedience*,
or Marcello of the prologue to *The Conformist* (in a
recent interview he resolutely denied the presence of any
direct autobiographical reference in his work). But
certainly, on this and later occasions, Moravia allows

a brief moment of tenderness to appear in his portrayal of childhood, a period of life which adult memory recalls with compassion.

Meanwhile, immediately after the publication of *The Time of Indifference*, Moravia began to travel. In spite of his journeyings, however, he managed to work methodically. Some years earlier, from the time when he had begun to write *The Wheel of Fortune* he had acquired the habit of writing every morning from nine to midday. Afterwards, the author remarked on several occasions, it was to this almost bureaucratic regularity that he owed the fact that he succeeded in writing a lot without working much. He was not only working at his new novel and at the short stories, but was also writing articles for newspapers. He went to England in 1930 for *La Stampa*, and later to several other countries. He stayed in London and Paris from 1930 to 1935. In England he had occasion to admire "that virile and courageous people,"[1] and to suffer hunger: "But you do get hungry there! I wonder how one can work on that diet. I like to eat well; I would go mad!"[2] Nothing interested the young writer more than his visits, in 1930, to the London *salon* of Lady Ottoline Morrel, who was able to indulge herself in inviting to dinner, all at the same time, men like H. G. Wells, W. B. Yeats, E. M. Forster, Bertrand Russell, and Lytton Strachey. Unfortunately, Moravia was too late to meet Joseph Conrad, who was very friendly with Lady Ottoline.

Although he was employed as foreign correspondent, relations between Moravia and the Fascist Government were getting worse. He was officially accused of being an immoral writer. In fact he was now associating with anti-Fascists, and this had leaked out. In an interview with *Les Nouvelles Littéraires* in 1947, Moravia gave some general opinions about Fascism which throw light upon the atmosphere of that period:

Fascism, for me, is a nightmare. It is difficult to explain. You have endured for four years a foreign occupation that could perhaps give you an idea of it, but it's not the same thing. It is less terrible because, when all's said and done, it is not a foreign occupation, and it's worse because certain bonds, even relations of sympathy, grew up between you and the Fascists, which is impossible with a foreign invader. In short, a dictatorship breathes, and the greatest danger is that of adaptation. We were cut off, and so the writers who stayed here seem new in Europe, because they were unable to make themselves known. Vittorini, for example, Alvaro, Piovene and others. Whereas Silone, who was in Switzerland, was able to take his due place.[3]

In July 1935, when *The Wheel of Fortune* originally appeared, an order suddenly came from the Ministero della Cultura Popolare not to discuss the book, and at the same time the writer lost his appointment with the *Gazzetta del popolo*. In the autumn of that same year, he left for the U.S.A.

Pancrazi[4] notes how the critics, having spoken of the immorality of *The Time of Indifference* when it was first published, soon began to speak of the author's moralising attitude. Nor was this all. By degrees, they began to portray and represent him "almost as a censor and a corrector of public morality in a corrupt age."[5] In other words, they said, the writer, leaving out nothing of what accompanies and follows the drama of evil, achieves his aim of dissuading the reader from taking the same path. But, continues Pancrazi:

Moravia sensibly lent an attentive and a rather favourable ear to these critics, and thereby gained both benefits and handicaps. In the novels and the short stories which followed (*The Wheel of Fortune* [1935], "The Happy Life" [1935] and "The Im-

broglio" [1937]) the moral element began to be introduced with greater self-consciousness. The misconception of Moravia the corrupter vanished, even for
the slowest and most timorous readers.[6]

This observation is certainly valid for *The Wheel of
Fortune*, whose very title (*Le ambizioni sbagliate* in Italian
—*i.e.* "Mistaken Ambitions") revealed the moralistic
intentions of the author. In fact, *The Wheel of Fortune*
still explores, only in a different dimension, that world
which belongs to *The Time of Indifference*, and which had
also partly constituted the formula of its success: the
unceasing and merciless struggle for life; the lack of
trust and friendliness amongst men who see in their
neighbours only a means towards their own gain; and
the consequent isolation of the individual. But here
Moravia is perfunctorily seeking effects in the wake of
the success of the first novel. He crudely piles on the
colour, and ends by prejudicing the validity of the work.

Pietro, Andreina, Maria Luisa, Stefano Davico, all
ambitious in different ways, for money, their careers,
their social position, are nightmarish characters who try
very hard to develop their absurd roles: all acting as if
under an evil spell, they are all to some degree accom-
plices in the final crime. The range of their emotions is
reduced to purely negative feelings: honesty for them
is always a form of collective hypocrisy, because otherwise it would never be able to be more than a synonym
for misfortune. Everything is basically genuine in substance, but is projected into a distorted dimension,
where one may discuss a murder in the same way that
one discusses a sea-trip.

No one is spared. A few of the minor characters,
Matteo and Carlino, for example, with their moments
of ingenuous humaneness, creep into the spotlight of the
story only to be hurled back again in ridicule to the
margin of life, to realise with profound disappointment

the stupidity of their behaviour, out of place in the shining circle of ambition pressing on them from all sides. Conceived strictly in terms of a moral judgment which pre-exists them, all the characters of *The Wheel of Fortune* end up fixed in a single dimension, where obscenity, hate, and betrayal rouse no horror and do not result from some kind of animal innocence, but are expressed with the mechanical gestures of automata.

Naturally, ambition (which is the *deus ex machina* of the novel) plays every possible trick on those who are foolish enough to trust it: the schemes of action which each of these ambitious people has conceived strictly to his own advantage are thwarted and diverted in other directions by the most incredible crossings and clashes with the plans of the other principal characters. Moravia's interest in plot, already displayed in *The Time of Indifference*, becomes excessive here: the number of strands it gathers together and artificially co-ordinates is such that, at a certain point, instead of assisting the reading by creating suspense, it makes the novel muddled and indigestible. Not only this, but the surfeit of unexpected happenings, the most disconcerting and incredible intertwinings of situations, the twists, the misunderstandings, the failure to distinguish primary and secondary levels in the plot—all the narrative apparatus which stands between the comedy of errors and the nineteenth-century novel, with the influence of the detective story in addition—reduce the drama to the grotesque.

This lengthy novel of five hundred packed pages, in which Moravia had sought to improve on the success of *The Time of Indifference*, is a failure. Its lack of organisation is the result of Moravia's acrobatic attempts to control his super-abundant material. It is obvious that the author has entered into his characters from the outside—not by the main road of truth, but along the byways of sophistry. But one positive quality is also obvious: even if these characters exist in one dimension, fixed in one idea or one extreme attitude, they never disappear from the page, leaving only their names behind. It is easy to see a better characterisation in *The Wheel of Fortune* and a greater robustness and substance of dialogue than in *The Time of Indifference*. If the novel lacks truth as a whole, it never lacks solidity in its single moments (see for example, the landscapes of anguish which fill it).

This brings up the question of style. In *The Wheel of Fortune*, even if sometimes the author abuses grammar and diction and achieves thereby a cacophony and a slovenliness which is decidedly irritating, the style still has, fundamentally, that force, originality, and freshness which has already been observed and which distinguishes all Moravia's prose. It is, in its seemingly impersonal tone, the style of the *Civil Code* of Stendhal or the *Twelve Tables* of Seneca. The fact that Moravia tends towards a kind of moral-writing which is descriptive, essay-like, social, rather than lyric (though there are in certain cases, such as *Agostino* and *Two Women*, high lyric tones), plainly implies the exact link between language and the precise reality which is its subject, thus falling short of, or rather lying beyond all literary complacency.

REFERENCES

1. Delpech, "A la télévision avec Moravia," 1948.
2. *Op. cit.*
3. *Les nouvelles littéraires*, 17 Apr. 1947.
4. Pancrazi *op. cit.*, pp. 110-15.
5. *Op. cit.*
6. *Op. cit.*

CHAPTER IV

PLOT TECHNIQUE

The Wheel of Fortune, and more particularly the collection of long short stories, *The Imbroglio*, which followed in 1937, provide useful examples of Moravia's plot technique, both in its significance and its limitation. Instead of speaking of "short stories," the critics (Debenedetti,[1] De Michelis[2]) have also spoken of "short novels," because of their length ("The Wayward Wife" is 84 pages long) and their structure, which has all the elements of a novel, for they are often virtually divided into chapters.

The technical and structural justification for their length is apparent: the short stories are long enough to permit a true interplay of plot and anecdote and to vary patterns of events and their developments, without the risk of the heavy and complicated machinery of *The Wheel of Fortune*, where the writer almost seems to lose control. On the cover flap, Moravia makes a few explicit statements to elucidate his intentions:

> The author has sought to give preponderant importance to the plot, because, if the short story is to rise again from its present stage of inferiority, compared with the novel, it must regain its former character, turn back to plot and anecdote, exploit its possibilities for violent *dénouements* and rapid syntheses and condense events into natural and concise narrative, in the same way as would be done by a man who is relating aloud events which have actually taken place.[3]

These stories, therefore, mark a return to tradition.

These encounters and clashes of events and people, in which the outer events provoke the internal drama of the characters, and constitute the charm of story-telling, have, in fact, an ancient, honourable position in Italian literature, from Boccaccio down to Goldoni's comedy of errors. But the author's statement gave the critics an opportunity to find fault with his unsophisticated technique. The tradition Moravia had followed appeared to represent a retrogression from the twentieth to the nineteenth century. "A mature storyteller. The most severe, indeed the only objection that one can make against him," observed Debenedetti[4] at the end of his well-reasoned essay, "is that he has not yet learnt how to create a novel without a certain adventure-story element." After Flaubert and the realists, who had already created a novel set in provincial society, devoid of any "stagey" elements in the plot, and after the dissolution of the traditional forms of nineteenth-century narrative carried out by Proust and Joyce, one can well understand the slightly scornful attitude of the critics. But we must go more closely into Moravia's meaning in the statement quoted above in order to show that the writer is at least not guilty of naïvety, but on the contrary, had known the full implications of his conservative attitude from the beginning.

Moravia's predilection for plot must, in the first place, be linked with his predilection for theatrical technique, already mentioned in connexion with *The Time of Indifference*. Moravia had, in fact, already remarked, with regard to *The Time of Indifference*, that his ambition had been "to apply to the novel the Aristotelian principle of the unities of time, place and action."[5] And he said later on that he had done this because he felt "the need to exert a firm hold on reality, which continually seemed to escape and melt away."[6] This recalls a remark by Fernandez, who noted how Moravia succeeds in the first place, through his "integral" style, in "her-

metically fixing the horizon of his problems."[7] At a
time when the sense of values and of relationships is
being lost, when the ground is being gradually prepared,
historically, for the disintegration of traditional style,
Moravia, far from attempting to repeat Joyce's unrepeatable experiment, felt "the need to exert a firm
hold on reality, which continually seemed to him to
escape and melt away."[8] That is, he felt the need to
harness facts and problems within a traditional narrative
technique which avoids asphyxia of expression, and
strives towards structural clarity. As we have seen with
The Time of Indifference, Moravia certainly used sensitive
feelers in detecting "that certain modern uneasiness" of
which Debenedetti spoke. But in Moravia's work that
uneasiness had found its expression and emphasis in
terms of contents, rather than in terms of technique.

Some years later, immediately after the publication
of *The Woman of Rome*, Moravia forestalled possible
criticism of the death of all the characters at the end of
the book as an error in technique, by saying in an article
called "Why I wrote *The Woman of Rome*"[9] that for
him this violence was not simply a meaningless convention. He had, in this, the precedent of *Hamlet*, where "at
the end of the tragedy all the characters are destroyed,
poisoned and bowled over like so many ninepins."[10]
Having explained that "the characters in dramas and in
dramatic novels die because the curve of their parabola
reaches its end, and death is merely the obvious final
point where the curve itself terminates,"[11] he observes
that since *The Woman of Rome* is not a naturalistic or a
realistic novel it does not have to obey the canons of
realism or naturalism, and he concludes by saying that
"no-one will say that 'natural' deaths in realistic novels
do not belong in their turn to a convention, though of
another kind."[12] This makes quite clear how Moravia
may even use plot technique as an almost surrealistic
device, without quite claiming a realism which is ac-

cessory and external, in the nineteenth-century sense. On the other hand, this same technique is unquestionably a limitation when, by its abuse, the plot shapes itself entirely in external scene-painting, irrelevant to the drama of the characters, and becomes the deliberate, intricate plan of a puppeteer. And yet, in an almost paradoxical way, this dynamic plot technique succeeds at times in *The Wheel of Fortune* in giving a firmer outline to the existentialist drama of the *bourgeois*. The characters, in fact, are determined by the trend of events (the casualness of a life without order and without aim) rather than by their will; and so, owing to the unexpectedness of the situations in which they find themselves, in conflict with other characters, they end by revealing their psychological motivation in a very clear light: as a person is shown from all sides by refracted light in a prism of mirrors.

REFERENCES

1. Debenedetti, "L'Imbroglio di Moravia," 1955, pp. 213-22.
2. De Michelis, *Introduzione a Moravia*, 1954.
3. *The Imbroglio*, 1935.
4. Debenedetti, *op. cit.*
5. Limentani, *op. cit.*, p. 30.
6. *Ibid.*
7. Fernandez, "Essai sur A.M.," in *Le Roman italien et la crise de la conscience moderne*, Paris 1958, pp. 9-138.
8. Limentani, *op. cit.*, p. 30.
9. In *Fiera Letteraria*, 3 Jul. 1947.
10. *Op. cit.*
11. *Op. cit.*
12. *Op. cit.*

CHAPTER V

FASCISM, SATIRE, ALLEGORY

1935, the year when *The Wheel of Fortune* was published, saw Moravia in New York. We do not know much of Moravia's life in America, or elsewhere for that matter. Where his private life is concerned, Moravia is unusually retiring and unco-operative with his critics. No sustained biographical study exists, and the general information available is very scanty. At any rate, with the exception of his illness, the difficult relations with Fascism and the long trips abroad, his life appears to be rather uneventful, devoted entirely to writing and working.

In New York Moravia taught Italian, we do not know where, to students who were "full of good will and curiosity."[1] He went to Mexico once, which was later to provide him with an exotic background for *The Fancy Dress Party*, the only novel, in spite of his travels, he set outside Italy. By now Moravia must have been fully aware of the gap that separated his view of life from that of contemporary, *bourgeois*, Fascist Italy. Moravia himself stated[2] later that he travelled a lot to avoid compromising too much with a boastful and dangerous reality.

Moravia's tales could hardly please the men who were successfully creating an image of a Great Society by shooting Abyssinians. Attempts were made to discourage the writer. The idea was that a strong people needed a strong literature, and Italian literature could not be "immoral," since the society it reflected was "moral." Moravia's expulsion from the *Gazzetta del Popolo* and the misfortunes of *The Wheel of Fortune* now frightened his publisher. When he received the new typescript of *The Imbroglio*, he informed the writer that he was very busy printing the memoirs of Marshal Badoglio (who had just emerged "victorious" from the so-called Abyssinian War) and, therefore, could not go ahead with the publication. Bompiani then became Moravia's publisher.

The six years of intensive work I dedicated to *Le Ambizioni Sbagliate*, a task I shall never repeat, for art should not be drudgery, did at least serve to loosen me up. For after that I wrote the five stories of *L'Imbroglio* in two months.[3]

The best is the one that gives its title to the book: the story of a naïve, generous man, the slightly ridiculous victim of the lady he is in love with—a confidence trickster. In the end he is repaid with the mature caress of his landlady. But the other stories are highly successful too: "La provinciale," "L'avaro," "L'architetto," and "La Tempesta." However, after the set-back of *The Wheel of Fortune* Moravia now seems cautious, as if intent on reconsidering his means of expression and finding some kind of reconciliation between *bourgeois* morals and the restless suffering, the paroxysm almost, of the accusations in the earlier books. The world around him now seems to have forced the writer's hand and he withdraws a little inside himself and even comes (almost unthinkably for Moravia) to optimistic conclusions, after the fashion of *bourgeois* narrative with its sentimental bias. But it would be doing Moravia an injustice to link *The Imbroglio* simply with a phase of withdrawal. The detachment with which the stories are set out, the broad sense of structure, the carefully gauged psychological observations, the new sense of colour and detail (for example, apart from the finely drawn characters, the care for geographical settings and accurate landscapes), in other words a more placid observation of reality, foreshadow the more complex and flexible world, the spacious canvases, of some of the works to follow.

However, when *The Imbroglio* was published in 1937, Moravia did not see its publication, having left in the meantime for China, where he stayed for two months. He went both ways by sea. His attempt to return via Siberia and Moscow failed. This was the period when the U.S.S.R. was crippled by the wave of terror which has gone down in history as the Great Purge. In the West, in the meantime, new societies, competing for material power, were brutally asserting themselves, drifting swiftly and surely towards another war. In Italy the anti-Fascists were being more and more closely watched. "The ten years between Hitler's rise to power and the fall of Fascism, 1933-1943," Moravia recalls, "were from the point of view of public life the worst years of my life, and even to-day I cannot recall them without horror. Perhaps that was why I travelled so much, to get away from an atmosphere poisoned by lies, fear, and conformity."[4]

Even though, for Moravia, travel was only second in importance to writing, contrary to the fashion of the time (one has only to think of the English and American writers living in Paris before the War), it was still exceptionally important in his formation. Although his literary horizon, as he says, never went beyond Lake Trasimene, his international experience always helped him to steer clear of the doldrums of provincial caricature. It also prevented him from being caught up in the vogue prevalent among Italian writers before and immediately after the War, for imitating American literature without a first-hand knowledge of that country, and thereby creating a European myth of America. This imitation had been able to renew the stagnant waters of our narrative writing; but, in some cases, it was verging on a new form of aestheticism, because of its

over brusque and rather abstract virulence. "I went to
China," Moravia said in 1937

for the same reason as I travelled in Europe and
America, in order not to follow the trend towards
aestheticism, which seems to me to be a characteristic
of provincialism. I mean that in two or three of these
trips you can free yourself of the most obvious influence from beyond the frontier, and so rid your
mind of some prejudices either for or against things
foreign, which are those most dangerous to the aims
of a really responsible culture. On the other hand,
leaving one's own country allows one to get a fairer,
more rounded idea of it than that of someone who has
not the courage to tear himself away.[5]

Moravia makes many such accusations against
Italian provincialism and reactionary conservatism,
throughout the essays, articles and interviews which
provide a kind of critical counterpoint to his creative
writing. His social interest seems to have become more
acute recently, with his writing for magazines and newspapers, and this is also to be attributed to the new
atmosphere of "commitment" in which Italian post-war
intellectuals live. Books like *Two Women* are very important documents in this field. Meanwhile, however,
it was with the collection of stories "I sogni del pigro"
(*A Lazy Man's Dreams*, 1940), "L'Epidemia" (*The
Epidemic*, 1944) and the novel *The Fancy Dress Party*
(1941), that Moravia became decisively and objectively
aware of the need for, or at any rate the possibility of,
some kind of critical realism.

Sanguineti writes that

the opposition between rich and poor, which in
Moravia both hides and exposes the class struggle,
has never been so vividly expressed as it is in the
brilliant satire of *The Epidemic*, the "Primo rapporto
sulla terra dell' inviato speciale della luna," ["First

report on the earth by the special envoy from the moon"], where the psychology of Fascism is expressed with the incomparable stylisation of caricature. When the economic causes are ignored, the earth becomes a 'strange country' inhabited by two races well defined 'both morally, and to some extent physically: the race of men called rich and that of men called poor'; two races distinguished by certain mysterious paradoxical characteristics. The poor, for example, 'do not like cleanliness and beauty' but 'by some strange perversion of taste' prefer 'rags to new clothes, council houses to villas and apartments, cheap furniture to good makes'; the poor 'do not like culture' and happily confuse the worst commercial products with the greatest masterpieces, do not go to museums, nor visit concert halls; the poor 'hate nature' and 'prefer municipal pools to the sea, dirty fields in the suburbs to the country, and the terraces of their houses to the mountains'; they like to live in sordid tenements, they enjoy 'turning clods of earth with crude heavy iron instruments', they plunge into coal-mines; they smoke bad tobacco, and as for their food, 'they do not like early vegetables, and wait until the peas are floury, the artichokes stringy, and the asparagus like wood before they eat them'; lastly, the poor mysteriously neglect their health, exposing themselves carelessly to all weathers and taking no care of themselves when they are ill 'because of their absurd passion not to miss a single day in the factories, the mines, or the fields.'[6]

Just an example but a significant one. Satire, allegory, the apologue, and the morality were the only possible ways open for social criticism under the Fascist régime. And this also explains the sentimental origin, based on human and not mere literary experience, of many stories, not only in *The Epidemic*, but also in *A Lazy*

Man's Dreams. And, at the same time in other stories, where the craftsman gets the upper hand, it explains the self-satisfaction, in a literary sense, of a prose that tends to become artificial and to delight in itself.

However, this tone of biting and vaguely unbalanced satire (the stories were called surrealistic and satirical) which does not always bear comparison with the illustrious names of Swift, Poe, Schwob, Leopardi, and La Bruyere, is at the core of the new novel, *The Fancy Dress Party*. Politically, this is the most violent caricature Moravia has written, and, together with *The Wheel of Fortune*, one of his worst books.

There had been a shift from the "unsuccessful tragedy" of *The Time of Indifference* to the "successful tragedy" of *The Wheel of Fortune*, ending in the comedy of parody in *The Fancy Dress Party*. The title itself has a specific meaning, for which the fancy dress party, in the Countess Gorina's house, which does not in fact take place, is only an ironic pretext. The real topic is a bitter and satirical parody of the Fascist régime and its principal figures: a society concealing the most despicable vices and depravities behind ancient virtues and costumes. One passes, therefore, from the obsessive sternness and solemnity of *The Wheel of Fortune* to the fanciful playfulness of *The Fancy Dress Party*, a brilliant literary exercise. It is clear that anyone who accuses Moravia of treating the subject coldly and dispassionately has misunderstood the book's essential character of hard moral judgment, from which no one can escape. Indeed, here the unrestrained use of intrigue is necessary not just to entertain but as the very means of expression. And, therefore, it is not literary and artificial. Men living in a world of isolation and tedium, as the Fascists did, exist only in an atmosphere of complexity and coincidence, there is no spontaneous meeting of souls. The externals of the plot simply reflect the tortuousness of the psychological movements.

In contrast with the "truth" of Michele (who still moves in a dimension that is completely human and accessible to us, because he suffers inwardly the schism between the dream of a better reality, and the reality that is being shaped around him historically) here we have characters completely focused in one of their one-dimensional limits of "beliefs" and "concrete" actions: beliefs and actions inevitably twisted and mystified by the "events" which result from them. Theatricality, drama, fiction, and disguise are therefore the concrete and necessary symbols of a disintegration of values, reflected in a narrative style. When the "innocent land" of the dream fades away, the hope of an ultimate moral dignity in dealings with the world fades with it, only the farce of life remains. And up to this point all is well. But the author ends up by exaggerating the mechanical dynamism of the individual's relationship with reality, so that in the end everything seems quite "discoloured, banal, hurried, composed as mechanically as a traditional serial story."[7] It also means all too often that in *The Fancy Dress Party* Moravia forgets to assume the role of a surgeon, for whom the scalpel is a double-edged instrument, difficult to handle. In conclusion, Russo was near the mark when he wrote that, behind the adventures of a South American:

the book describes the adventures of a dictator in our own country. The parallelism of the characters, and of their followers, the Chorus, is impressive and appropriately biting; the intrigues and construction are the satiric invention of one who affects admiration for the fashionable detective novel. Only the ending of the novel disturbs us, unexpectedly, like a vulgar serial story; here is a kind of Saverio da Montepin, who suddenly assumes the attitude of a moralist and satirist. But then, we wondered, isn't this Moravia always playing a little with his intellect and integrity, if he can fall into such cheap journalese?[8]

However, the reply of the censorship was not long in coming. After many and various mishaps (it seems that it actually ended up in Mussolini's hands) the novel was withdrawn from circulation in the second edition. At the same time the author was forbidden to sign newspaper articles with his own name. Moravia chose the "transparent pseudonym"[9] of Pseudo, and continued writing.

But he now seemed to hold himself aloof. *A Lazy Man's Dreams*, *The Epidemic*, *The Fancy Dress Party* had added little to his reputation as a novel writer. His finest book still remained the first one, *The Time of Indifference*, and critics of Moravia's works began to see in the novelist the one-book writer who more or less repeats himself. Moravia still had only a very limited public, and their eyes were attentive only to the erotic scenes, which the critics judged an end in themselves, deftly manipulated by a novelist looking for his public. While the world was sinking deeper and deeper into the terrible nightmare of the War, and in Italy itself conditions were becoming ever more favourable for the civil war of 1943, Moravia seemed to consolidate his position in a world of his own, the closed world of a writer who rejects all contact with the march of events, intent on minor works, almost on literary ornamentation. In actual fact, in the silence of his isolation he was allowing himself no respite: each problem that might concern his activity was faced with his accustomed seriousness, and the works that followed were the fruit of a long, difficult period of maturation. To understand this one need only consider some of the articles which were published at that time under the signature of Pseudo in the review *Prospettive*, edited by Curzio Malaparte. Here for example, is an extract from a long essay, dating from the period after 1941, entitled "L'uomo e il personaggio" ("Man and Character"). With admirable lucidity and a critical eye for essentials, Moravia puts forward considerations concerning the crisis of man, and therefore of character, in the contemporary novel, which have now become generally accepted. After he has observed and discussed the fact that no nineteenth-century writer had ever doubted that he was concerned with an objective reality, so that he could simply place himself in front of reality in an attitude of study, research, and examination (this attitude was to find its canonisation in the "truth" of the naturalists, a "truth" that soon "showed itself as false, utterly false, no less false than the *papier mâché* tragedies of late neoclassical drama, or than the last epics")[10] he then goes on to talk at length about this dissolution of character, from Stendhal, Balzac, Flaubert, Zola, Austen, Brontë, Thackeray, Dickens, Gogol and Tolstoy to Dostoevsky, Proust and Joyce. It is worth quoting generously, because the extract will help towards a better understanding of much of Moravia's output, especially his later work:

Parallel to Proust, Joyce exhausts the formula of naturalism by showing that a character immediately ceases to exist once the heterogeneous elements of which he is composed have been analysed. His character Bloom is not a man, but rather a crossroads at which the most varied and incomprehensible traffic intersects. He is richer than anyone else, because he is able to think, feel and be the most varied things, and at the same time he is poorer than anybody else, because he lacks a centre round which this tumultuous material can be arranged. Setting out from the same impressionism, both Proust and Joyce break up their characters to an extent which is fatal: the first into the changing flow of time, and the second into a mass of objects registered by the conscious mind. With these writers the character swells, expands beyond human boundaries, it is Time itself passing, the mass of things that exist and seek order. These two writers can without doubt be considered the final points of the nineteenth-century novel, and at the same time the initiators of the modern novel. . . .

Clearly this crisis of character corresponds to a similar crisis in the concept of man. Modern man seems a mere cipher within mass groupings which are amongst the most formidable humanity has ever known. He does not exist for himself, but as part of something else, of an organism, a sentiment, a collective concept. It is very difficult to make a character out of such a man, at least in the traditional meaning of the word. And indeed the characters of the modern American novel which, contrary to popular belief, continues in a way the post-naturalist traditions of the last century, are atomic in stature, embryonic, elementary. Or else they are symbolic, summarising collective conditions or ideologies. The film, creator of faces and attitudes in two dimensions, exerts a notable influence on this novel; and so does journalism. The American novel, in short, is still the most vital because it has remained the most faithful to the ancient premises of the novel at all times. But it is not yet clear if it is a rearguard or a vanguard.[11]

REFERENCES

1. Delpech, "A la télévision avec Moravia," 1948.
2. Accrocca, *op. cit.*
3. Del Buono, *op. cit.*, p. 38.
4. Accrocca, *op. cit.*
5. Limentani, *op. cit.*, p. 85.
6. Sanguineti, *op. cit.*, p. 13.
7. Guarnieri, "A.M.," 1955.
8. Russo, "A.M.," 1958.
9. Accrocca, *op. cit.*
10. *Prospettive*, 1941.
11. *Op. cit.*

CHAPTER VI

REPRESENTATIONAL ASPECTS OF MORAVIA'S ART: WAR AND THE EXPERIENCE OF THE PEOPLE

The excerpt from Moravia's essay quoted at the end of the preceding chapter illustrates perfectly the situation in which the novelist found himself. After the extreme and sensational attempt by Proust and Joyce to capture all the possible dimensions of reality, different ways lay open to Moravia. He could try once more to represent as complete a dimension of man as possible, necessarily experimenting with new techniques of expression. In the long run this would have led, in his own words, "to asphyxia, or to a new baroque style which no longer has any content."[1] Alternatively, he could reduce the character to Hemingway's embryonic, symbolic dimension; or else he could compromise, by giving as realistic a picture as possible of characters without identity, by means of a traditional, representational technique. This is the way Moravia chose: a way that led him, through *Agostino, Disobedience, Conjugal Love, A Ghost at Noon* (a very un-Moravian English title for a book called *Il Disprezzo (Contempt)* in Italian), to the massive attempt of *The Empty Canvas.*

Of course, to give form to a character's crisis, whilst retaining the representational dress and traditional language, the character must be constructed, however embryonically, according to the scheme of a guiding idea. Moravia himself pointed out, in an article which appeared in April 1956,[2] how even Proust and Joyce make attempts to order their reality according to an ideology of some kind. "Why ideology?," he asks, and replies: "Because even when it seems sophisticated and perhaps useless, as in Proust, or unnecessary and literary, as in Joyce, it still appears to re-establish the language of reason which itself is universal, and hence a connexion of some kind between the writer and reality."

If, by ideology, we understand "living essence of facts"[3] without other superimposed values (political, religious, psychological, etc.), and if we consider how Moravia tends to turn literature into a diagnostic instrument of research and "communication," it is easy to understand the following observation, which is clearly also a protest against those who accuse the writer of abusing the sexual *motif* in his novels:

My concentration on the sexual act, which is one of the most primitive and unalterable motives in our relation to reality, is due precisely to this urgency; and the same can be said of my consideration of the economic factor, which is also primitive and unalterable, in that it is founded on the instinct of self-preservation that man has in common with animals. . . . Our opponent will then ask why it seems necessary to talk at all about the sexual act in modern literature. To this my simple reply is that sex in the modern world is synonymous with love. Who can deny that love is a very frequent subject in the literature of all times and all places? But, someone will say, has love been transformed into sex in modern literature, that is to say, has it lost the indirect, metaphorical and idealised character it had in the past, and so ended up by being identified with the sexual act? The reasons for this identification are many; the chief one is the decline in the taboos and prohibitions which too often compelled false idealisations of the erotic act in an artificial way.[4]

To conclude: "I am probably a monotonous writer

always saying the same things, rather like certain birds who repeat the same tune; but from time to time changing the way in which I see these things."[5]

Money and sex, the two constant poles between which *bourgeois* and neo-capitalist society move, are then, in the writings of Moravia the only basic criteria for every judgment about human and social reality, for every interpretation of existence. In a world populated by men who tend to reduce the reasons for their existence to the most rudimentary skeleton, the only realities that we cannot reduce farther are sex and money. This is the writer's extreme attempt to find a physiognomy that can still be checked against the data of experience for men in our time, trapped as they are in the vicious circle of a race without winning posts. Within this context Moravia takes up an attitude peculiar to him: he always attacks the character first of all from the outside, almost as if a minute description of the body could indicate in some manner a way of approach to the soul. As in Joyce's portrayal of Bloom, the character is reduced by now "to a crossroads at which the most incomprehensible traffic intersects."[6] It is as if in the last resort all the good and evil, or better the chaos that is within, could para- doxically find its expression in a mould, in a corporeal mask. "For few other novelists," observes Debenedetti

is the phrase 'to put flesh on a character' so literal and pertinent. In Moravia each figure is born, or at least presents itself, under a prevailing aspect of physic- ality. And it is a special, circumscribed physicality, more properly called carnality. The spirit or soul or whatever stands for them is seen primarily in the im- print, or stigma that they have pressed into the flesh. The first reaction to each character—the first aspect of that vice, or mania, or passion or weakness that will expose him to the crisis—always emerges from the representation of a physical trait, on which the eye of the narrator immediately fastens. And even if this trait needs concealing less than any other, it is still revealed in every case with a sort of wanton bitterness that exposes the nakedness when the veil has been torn away.[7]

While Moravia was so actively engaged, in essays and polemics, in seeking critically his dimension as a writer, in estimating his own means and in preparing himself for his future works, Italy was rushing headlong into the long tragedy of the last two years of the War. The Fascist Government had collapsed on 25 July 1943. But, after a brief interlude of chaotic tension, Mussolini was freed by the Germans, and towards the end of September he proclaimed a Fascist republic in the north of Italy. The first collapse, amidst the enthusiasm and derision of the people, and the ever present threat of a final collapse suddenly made the small surviving band of believers in Mussolini's dream extremely dangerous. This was the beginning of the civil war in Italy.

Moravia who, like so many others after 25 July, had published two violently anti-Fascist articles in the *Popolo di Roma*, knew he was included in the list of people who were to be arrested, and so he was forced to flee. "From the innocuous polemics of 1929 to the flight of 1943 to save my skin"[8] the parabola of Moravia's relations with the Fascist dictatorship had come to an end. The writer fled towards Naples, but he did not succeed in crossing the frontier, and he retired to live in a stable near Fondi, in the mountains of Ciociaria, a little to the north of the front on the Garigliano. This too was a violent, unwanted experience which was to bear fruit in *Two Women*.

I had an experience which usually intellectuals don't have. I lived with peasants, ate their food, slept with them, stayed with them all day. So I conceived a great interest in the people, the people who work hard. After the war I stayed on for a year in the mountains and by the time I came back to Rome I had a certain sympathy with them, particularly because at that time, 1945-6, Italy was in a very bad condition. Even the rich suffered from hardship, but the poor were paying for everybody, as usual. So I tried to write about them. I wrote four books about ordinary people—two books of "Roman Tales", in all 130 short stories, and two novels, *Two Women* and *The Woman of Rome*. The heroes of those books, two simple women from the people who spoke in their simple way, and the short stories about workmen who spoke in the first person—they were a kind of relief for me as a writer because I like to create people who are morally healthy and very simple, and who like to talk about their own affairs. But now it is exhausted —my experience in the mountains. I have gone back to the intellectuals in my last novel, for its hero is a painter, highly sophisticated. For the moment, anyway, I have left simple people. To make simple people talk I had to create a style which was fresh at first, but has now become rather mannered. I'm tired of it. I must have the feeling of freshness in my work. Nothing mannered.[9]

Let us briefly examine this new line-up: Moravia and the working class.

"They were a kind of relief for me as a writer, because I like to create people who are morally healthy and very simple and who like to talk about their own affairs."[10] That was how Moravia put it. But this is really a piece of polemic simplification. In actual fact, Moravia's relationship with the working class was never to be exactly idyllic. Even the most balanced of his ordinary people, Adriana in *The Woman of Rome* (and note that here we have the extreme case of Moravia's love for the people) is to be understood primarily as a critical term of comparison, here with a few sentimental touches added, for use in the diagnosis of the malaise of the *bourgeoisie*. In other words, here, and even more with the characters of the Roman proletariat or sub-proletariat, whose vices and weaknesses are almost caricatured, it is not really a question of a positive, constructive sympathy for the people, but more of a wholly negative, forced sympathy, originating in Moravia's fierce and persistent hatred for the *bourgeois* class. In the same way an artist does not necessarily paint a white background out of a particular love of white, but merely to set the dark colours of his picture in strong relief. Mino remarks in *The Woman of Rome*: "The rich are appalling but the poor certainly aren't any better, if for different reasons."[11] "Reasons" for which, of course, the *bourgeois* are responsible, and which allow the people to be diagnosed in terms of an instinctive innocence exhausted by reality. " 'In the abstract' [it is still Mino speaking] 'when I'm not among them I don't hate them; at least, I hate them so little that I believe in their progress. If I didn't believe this I wouldn't trouble myself with politics. But when I'm among them they horrify me. Really,' he added sadly, 'mankind is worthless.' "[12]

In Moravia, therefore, the working class and the intellectuals are naturally the only two possible instruments in the diagnosis of that *bourgeois* world of which they form the periphery; both caught at the moment of their bitterest struggle, and of course doomed to failure: on the one hand the people, trying to fulfil the dream of the *bourgeois* "paradise"; on the other the intellectuals, who experience that paradise as "hell," while they are living their hour of agony and alienation. Consider Adriana:

I told myself positively that I ought to make it my aim in life to live one day in a house like that, have a family like that, and live in that same way, which seemed to reveal the presence of innumerable firm and constant affections.[13]

And we next see her in a conversation with Mino, the student she is in love with:

"I would have liked" I said slowly, savouring the phrases in each of which one of my most cherished dreams seemed to be embodied "to have been just what you are so unhappy at being—I would have liked to have been born into a family as well-to-do as yours—I would have liked to have good teachers, foreign governesses, as you had—I would have liked to have spent the summer at the seaside or in the mountains—and to have had good clothes, and to be invited and to receive guests—and then I would have liked to marry someone who loved me, a decent fellow who worked and was well-to-do—and I would have liked to live with him and bear his children."

We were lying on the bed as we talked. Suddenly he leapt upon me, as was his way, clutching me and shaking me as he repeated: "Hurray, hurray, hurray! In fact, you'd have liked to be like Signora Lobianco."

"Who is Signora Lobianco?" I asked, both offended and disconcerted.

"A terrible harpy who often invites me to her receptions in the hope that I'll fall in love with one of her terrible daughters and marry her, because I'm what's called a good match."

"But I wouldn't like to be at all like Signora Lobianco!"

"But that's what you'd certainly be if you had all the things you mentioned. Signora Lobianco was born into a wealthy family that gave her an excellent education, with good teachers and foreign governesses, sent her to school and even to the University, I believe—she, too, grew up in a lovely clean house—she, too, went to the seaside or the mountains every summer—she, too, had beautiful clothes and was invited out and gave parties—lots of invitations and lots of parties—she, too, married a decent fellow, Lobianco the engineer, who works and brings a great deal of money into the house—and she has a number of children by this husband of hers, to whom I even believe she has been faithful—three daughters and a son—but despite all this she's a terrible harpy, as I said."

"She might be a harpy quite independently of her surroundings."

"No, she is one like her friends and the friends of her friends."[14]

However, Moravia's experience of the "people" bore fruit. Indeed, the first pages of *Two Women* were written in Rome in 1944, immediately after the intense experience the writer went through on the mountains of Ciociaria. Moravia's somewhat aesthetic deviation in *The Epidemic*, which appeared at this time, and in *A Lazy Man's Dreams*, was swept away forever. The best example of this refined narrative art, which concentrates on psychological investigation, is almost certainly the splendid short story entitled "The Unhappy Lover". This also provides the title, in 1943, for a collection of nine short stories, some of which had already been published in *The Happy Life*. Here again the subject is one of Moravia's many "conflicts" between man and woman, arising from a cruel and almost absurd lack of understanding, and set against sea scenes and sun-drenched beaches, utterly desolate in the isolation of the two protagonists who are living out the last phases of a love that has vanished forever.

1944, then, saw the beginning of *Two Women*. But, after ten pages, the writer presumably realised that the world of peasants and terrors that he wanted to depict was too near, too compelling, to allow him to be ob-

jective about it. It had not yet matured in him, his
feelings were too strong. The consequence of this was a
further endeavour towards social awareness in the book-
let *La Speranza* (*Hope*, written in 1944), which is a
kind of historical note on Christianity and Communism,
a Communism that is seen as Utopia and hope. The
essay is not very solid but it is stimulating; it is worked
out in a "professorial," "scholarly" style, as Russo says,
"in the style of a writer of brilliant text books, which
makes us admire his ability yet again."[15] But, Russo
went on, "we are inclined to believe that Moravia plays
the role of a Communist with the same slightly scholastic
flair which he produced years ago in playing the part
of a moralist in *A Lazy Man's Dreams*. He is indeed a
Communist, but in his narrative art, where perhaps he
himself does not realise it."[16] And at the same time as
La Speranza, he wrote his second great book, *Agostino*,
with the "all-consuming dream," the hope of the "unknown paradise," the "innocent land" of Agostino, in the
antinomy between "history" and "nature."

REFERENCES

1. Del Buono, *op. cit.*, p. 179.
2. "Note sul romanzo," 1956.
3. *Op. cit.*
4. Del Buono, *op. cit.*, p. 25.
5. *Ibid.*
6. *Prospettive*, 1941.
7. Debenedetti, *op. cit.*, pp. 213-22.
8. Accrocca, *op. cit.*
9. *The Guardian*, 31 May 1962
10. *Op. cit.*
11. *W.R.*, p. 295.
12. *Ibid.*
13. *W.R.*, p. 14.
14. *W.R.*, p. 293-94.
15. Russo, *op. cit.*
16. *Op. cit.*

CHAPTER VII

AGOSTINO

Almost all the critics, from Falconi to Fernandez, Flora and Gadda, who have written on *Agostino* (*Two Adolescents*), have always laid primary stress on the book's sexual theme, the awakening of an adolescent to sexual life. "What is this short novel?" asks Gadda. "It is the confrontation of Agostino, a thirteen year old boy, from a family 'of some standing', with the facts and problems of sex. Agostino, the only son of a widowed and attractive mother, 'undergoes' the discovery of sex."[1]

This young middle-class boy, Agostino, spends a few days by the sea one summer with his mother, a young and beautiful widow. Agostino is at first presented as proud and jealous of his mother, above all proud; then, as time goes by, jealous and unhappy. His mother strikes up a friendship with a young gigolo. A storm springs up in Agostino's young heart, a storm which will gather and suddenly burst forth within a short space of time. But another fact helps to bring the crisis to a head: Agostino's meeting with a gang of working-class boys on another part of the beach—Berto, Tortima, and others. In the centre, a symbol of depravity and the *deus ex machina* of every heartless and vulgar action or thought, stands the six-fingered homosexual beach attendant Saro, with his delicate querulous lover, the negro Homs. This chorus provides the counterpoint to Agostino's sexual initiation, which, even on the day his mother goes out on a beach raft with the friend she has picked up, had gone no deeper than suspicion. From Saro's gang, in fact, in the most brutal way possible,

M E

through explicit, mimic methods of description (with his mother as the object of the demonstration at the centre of the farce), Agostino becomes aware of the reality of sex, which until then had remained clouded over and buried in the depths of his consciousness. Everything now appears to him in a fresh perspective, and it is more than he can stand. The crisis reaches its climax and plunges him into a state of morbid confusion. Erotic fantasies now accompany his mother's appearance, her every gesture and movement. His attitude towards his mother is not determined by a definite Oedipus complex, but rather by a morbid, disconcerting attraction which tends to confirm the truth of the facts told him by Saro's gang, and which carries with it that disturbing feeling of rancour and bitterness, that desire for vengeance felt by someone who has until then been duped. His mother, on the other hand, now both mother and woman, the very essence of provocation in her casual domestic behaviour (to her Agostino remains an innocent little boy of thirteen), is the only woman with whom the child can come into close contact. It is precisely this superimposition of mother and alluring woman, this danger of giving way to an Oedipic kind of desire, which is to drive Agostino, in the company of Tortima, to seek admission to the local brothel. "If he could only possess one of those women . . . it would for ever . . . sever the thin thread of perverted and troubled sensuality which still bound him to his mother."[2] Turned away because of his short trousers, and after a clumsy, ineffective attempt to explain things to his mother, Agostino finds himself thrown back harshly into his new loneliness—the loneliness of an adolescent now aware of things around him—and the novel ends as follows, seemingly without a solution:

"Why do you want to go away?" she asked again. "Don't you like being with me?"

selves. He began wearing his oldest and dirtiest clothes, to the great surprise of his mother, who noticed that he no longer took any pride in his appearance; he made a point of never mentioning his luxurious home, and he took an ostentatious pleasure in ways and habits which up to that time had disgusted him. . . .

But . . . he really had changed. Without being conscious of it himself, without really trying to, he had, by dint of spending so much time with the boys every day, ended up by becoming very much like them, and had lost his old tastes without really acquiring new ones. More than once, in a mood of revolt against Bagno Vespucci, he had joined in the more innocent games of Bagno Speranza, seeking out his playmates of earlier in the summer. But how colourless and dull those nicely brought up boys now seemed to him, how boring their regulation walks under the eye of parents or tutors, how insipid their school gossip, their stamp collections, books of adventure and such like. The fact is that the company of the gang, their talk about women, their thieving expeditions in the orchards, even the acts of oppression and violence of which he himself had been a victim, had transformed him and made him intolerant of his former friendships.[6]

Sanguineti remarks that:

no one in our narrative literature has ever expressed better than Moravia this bitter fascination. It is not, as we are wont to say, and as the author himself would like to believe, the fascination of corruption or of perversion, but the fascination of life which judges us and harshly reveals us to ourselves. No one, to be more exact, has more effectively described, in direct narrative, the fatal masochism of the *bourgeois* who is incapable of spontaneous self-awareness; who is

accused of being precisely what he is, namely alienated
in an artificial, unnatural world, lacking true vitality
or authentic resistance, the *bourgeois* who, genuinely
corrupted at heart, finally recognises himself and
enjoys the very ruthlessness with which he is at least
isolated in his true condition and explained to himself.[7]

There is also another side to the story. At a certain
point, as we have seen, a more concrete and vital contact
with reality seems possible for Agostino only through
the gang's world; but those same boys in the gang,
intimidating and violent, on the fringe of lawlessness,
are themselves alienated from life in their turn, though
in a different way, or rather, in a totally opposite way
from Agostino. Each of these boys, in his harsh struggle
for life, has become an enemy to himself, to others and
to nature. Moreover, all of them are fired with an envy
which has turned to a grudging, dogged hatred against
anyone like Agostino, who already knows—and without
having "earned" it—their "unknown paradise," namely
the "*bourgeois* hell." Take the following passage for
example:

Tortima seemed to be struggling with an idea which
he could not succeed in formulating. At last he said:
"But supposing I was to appear at one of these receptions, and say: 'I've come too.' What would you
do?" As he spoke he got up and marched forward
impudently, with his hands on his hips and his chest
stuck out. The boys burst out laughing. "I should ask
you to go away," said Agostino simply, emboldened
by the laughter of the boys.
  "And supposing I refused to go away?"
  "I should ask our men to turn you out."
  "Have you got menservants?"
  "No, but my mother hires waiters when she has a
reception."

"Tuh, just like your father." One of the boys was evidently the son of a waiter.

"And supposing I resisted, and broke the waiter's nose for him and marched into the middle of the room and shouted 'You are a lot of rogues and bitches the whole lot of you.' What would you say?" insisted Tortima, advancing threateningly upon Agostino, and turning his fist round and round, as if to let him smell it. But this time they all turned against Tortima, not so much from a wish to protect Agostino as from a desire to hear more details of his fabulous wealth.

"Leave him alone . . . they'd kick you out, and a good thing too," was heard on all sides. Berto said sneeringly: "What have you got to do with it? Your father's a boatman and you'll be a boatman too; and if you did turn up at Pisa's [Agostino's nickname] house you certainly wouldn't shout anything. I can see you," he added getting up and mimicking Tortima's humility in Agostino's house. . . .

" 'Excuse me, is Mr. Pisa at home? Excuse me . . . I just came oh, he can't . . . Never mind, please excuse me . . . I'm sorry . . . I'll come another time.' Oh, I can see you. Why, you'd bow to the ground."

All the boys burst out laughing. Tortima, who was as stupid as he was brutal, didn't dare stand up to their taunts. But in order to get his own back he said to Agostino: "Can you make me an iron arm?"

"An iron arm?" repeated Agostino.[8]

Following this, still through the gang's hatred and sarcasm, Agostino discovers a further, two-sided alienation: his own absolute ignorance in matters of sex, resulting from a misguided education, and a contrasting degeneracy amongst the boys in the gang. For them, what in an improved society should be the Lawrencian purity of sex is naturally reduced (how it could possibly be otherwise is what Lawrence failed to ask himself) to a topic of obscene conversation.

"How do you mean, he doesn't know?" asked Tortima who hadn't understood.

"He just doesn't know," replied Saro simply. And turning to Agostino he said in a softer voice: "Speak up, Pisa. A man and a woman, what is it they do together? Don't you know?"

They all listened breathless. Agostino stared at Saro, who continued to smoke and watch him through half closed eyelids. He looked round at the boys, who were evidently bursting with stifled laughter, and repeated mechanically, through the cloud which seemed to cover his sight: "A man and a woman?"[9]

So Agostino does not know anything. He will have this repeated to him on all sorts of occasions and in the most varied tones, he will be mocked, ill-treated, beaten, humiliated, accused of pederasty, and he will fail to win the admiration of his companions, so much more versed and proficient than he in the organic, animal struggle for life which they conduct not so much on the level of everyday hypocrisy as on the level of open violence. Agostino will be rejected. But he will have learned a lesson in the meantime. He has not managed to become one of the wild band, but has fully understood the driving force of their actions and thoughts, just as he has had tangible experience once and for all of the falseness, the existential deformity, which is at the base of his own relationship to life.

A pasteboard world, padded with hypocrisy and money, is behind him. So well has he understood all this, so acutely does he feel the link between money and *bourgeois* morality, that, playing for a moment the part of a boatman's son, he is able to tear to pieces that selfsame world, here represented by a father and his "well brought up" little son, passengers during Agostino's boat-trip into the world of history, where the reality of class distinction and social relationships is very much alive. The father is given an opportunity of pointing out to his son a splendid example of good behaviour:

The man turned to his son and said to him probably half in fun: "There now Peter, give your ball to this boy who hasn't got one." The boy looked first at his father and then at Agostino, and greedily hugged his ball still tighter; but he still didn't say a word. "Don't you want to?" asked his father gently. "Don't you want to?"

"It's my ball," said the boy.

"Yes, it's yours, but if you like you may give it away," persisted the father. "This poor boy has never had one in all his life; now, don't you want to give it up to him?"

"No," said his son emphatically.

"Never mind," interposed Agostino at this point, with a sanctimonious smile, "I don't really want it. I shouldn't have time to play with it . . . it's different for him."

The father smiled at these words, pleased at having found such a useful object lesson for his son. "He's a better boy than you," he went on, stroking his son's head. "He's poor, but he doesn't want to take away your ball, he leaves it to you; but whenever you want to grumble and make a fuss I hope you'll remember that there are lots of boys like this in the world, who have to work, and who have never had a ball or any toys of their own."

"It's my ball," repeated the boy obstinately.

"Yes, it's yours" sighed his father, absent-mindedly. He looked at his watch and said in a tone of command: "It's time we went back; take us in, boy." Without a word, Agostino turned the prow towards the beach.[10]

"It's time we went back; take us in, boy." As Sanguineti points out, this is spoken " 'in a tone of command,' because the lesson is over and we are now going
back to reality, to good solid reality, and we must
make every effort to distinguish between this reality and
the moral lesson and, for heaven's sake, not confuse
them."[11]

In this way, with *Agostino*, the social theme has entered Moravia's work with full impact. Agostino has
now seen his own true face, mirrored in Piero's, and the
true face of his own mother in that of Piero's father. At
the same time, he has discovered the true faces of those
who are to provide the first example of Moravia's
"negative sympathy" for the proletariat. This finds full
expression in the *Roman Tales* and, almost in reactionary
terms, in the short story "Contact with the working
class" (1949). For Agostino the adventure of conscience
has begun. Yet what kind of adventure of conscience
can be experienced by someone who, whilst attempting
to break away from *bourgeois* existence, is entangled on
every side in the fine threads of its web and knows
only this form of existence? The self-respecting *bourgeois*
is every day jostled and assailed; despite all his mental
defences he is exposed every minute of the day to the
world around him, and the only respectable escape
open to him lies in the "dream" of a better world. Thus
this dream takes shape in the bitter conflict between our
everyday existence, and what we should like our existence to be; that is, between history and a dream that
can have no place in history. Thus, retreat or non-
participation is the last, sad remnant of moral dignity
which these nostalgic, impotent figures, deeply rooted
in a doomed class, can hope to attain.

The first person to bring to light this conflict between
"history" and "nature" in Agostino's mind was De
Michelis,[12] and this as early as 1954. Unfortunately, this
thesis is not developed coherently, but is left hanging

amidst diverse observations of an aesthetic, structural nature. Nevertheless, De Michelis shrewdly observes that the main theme of the novel is a recurrent theme in Moravia's work, an "unadorned, depairing elegy for youthful illusions destroyed at their first encounter with reality." He goes on to suggest that Agostino's age—he is thirteen, even younger than Gerolamo—is essential to Moravia's interpretation of youth. Moravia seems to be looking back, across the subsequent experiences which life has brought him, to a stage nearer the state of innocence. Youth is the sole source of relief from:

> the permanent state of oppression afflicting a person who begins to live under the domination of original sin. . . . But Agostino's thirteen years, as opposed to Gerolamo's seventeen and Michele's twenty, serve another purpose: to separate the character from the author, to help the author maintain his enquiry on a tone of judgment and pity, free from the narcissism of a position in which he could admit defeat whilst admiring his own cruelty; which is another way of saying the same thing, because it means telling the story of Agostino in the light of that longed for innocence, rather than in the light of his final inertia. . . .[13]

Agostino, like Michele, fails on the level of direct and vital relationships with his neighbour. His story, in fact, ends precisely where Michele's began, in the loneliness that is a result of alienation from every concrete and effective relationship with others. But Agostino is explicitly offered the new dream of the "innocent land" which is to determine his act of refusal and also be his source of consolation:

> [the] vague and desperate desire to ford the river and walk on and on down the coast, leaving far behind the boys, Saro, his mother, and all the old life. Who knows whether, if he were to go straight ahead and never turn back, walking, walking on the soft white

sand, he might not at last come to a country where none of these horrible things existed; a country where he would be welcomed as he longed to be and where it would be possible for him to forget all he had learned and then learn it again without all that shame and horror, gently and naturally as he dimly felt that it might be possible.[14]

Such an attitude is to become of central significance in the best of Moravia's later work.

REFERENCES

1. Gadda, "Agostino di A.M.," 1945.
2. A., in T.A., p. 68.
3. T.A., p. 83.
4. Flora, "A.M.," 1952, pp. 197-231.
5. Gadda, op. cit.
6. T.A., pp. 61-2.
7. Sanguineti, op. cit., pp. 62-3.
8. T.A., pp. 32-3.
9. T.A., p. 29.
10. T.A., p. 64.
11. Sanguineti, op. cit., p. 73.
12. De Michelis, op. cit.
13. Op. cit. p. 100
14. T.A., pp. 53-4.

CHAPTER VIII

THE WOMAN OF ROME

When *The Woman of Rome* appeared in 1947, eighteen years had already gone by since the publication of *The Time of Indifference*. Moravia's interests had gradually evolved along dual lines: a directly existentialist interest in the intellectual who is alienated from his own class, and an interest in social factors as they affect both the intellectual and the proletarian. In *Agostino* both of these elements had found vigorous expression. A simple psychological intuition had directed the powerful social investigation in *The Time of Indifference*: a book immersed in an atmosphere of desolation and of *bourgeois* corruption in which everything was distorted by sex (reduced to a vice) and money. Moravia's subsequent portrayal of men and passions was reinforced by a sense of social and historical values which was both extraordinarily imaginative and acute, and thus his intuition gradually acquired more precise cultural contours. The *motif* of money as the mould of character returns time and again to play a determining though subterranean role. And similarly the treatment of sex, as the only stable value in a world in dissolution, recurs constantly. At the same time, however, sex is often no longer an end in itself, nor even a means of salvation, but is reduced to a simple expedient by the pitiless organic economic struggle which torments us all, and finally degenerates into physical or mental vice. This is the case in *The Woman of Rome*, and even more clearly in *The Empty Canvas*. Some of the short stories—"L'avaro" ("The Miser"), "Ritorno dalla villeggiatura" ("Back from the

Holidays"), "Tired Courtesan"—provide striking examples of the way in which money is immediately and openly presented as the mainspring of the story. Apart from these, Gerolamo's inability to defend himself when confronted with the stimulations of life has already been depicted in "A Sick Boy's Winter," primarily in terms of the inexperience of a young *bourgeois* coming from an environment in which everything has been done for him at the expense of those who now become his tormentors. Moreover, some of the stories, "A Lazy Man's Dreams," "The Epidemic," and even *The Fancy Dress Party*, had already dealt with social problems.

But the book in which all the motivating forces of Moravia's work, from the social to the existential, are fused, is *The Woman of Rome*. Certainly *The Woman of Rome* is not a social novel, nor is it, in a strict sense, existentialist. Yet here, for the first time, a whole section of Italian society, that of the Fascists, is introduced into one of Moravia's books with high artistic accomplishment. The most varied types, from the intellectual to the politician, the mechanic, the prostitute, the murderer, are now brought face to face against the background of a complex and anonymous mass.

Thus *The Woman of Rome*, as a whole, can be considered one of Moravia's main novels. In a more complex way than *Agostino*, it is the point of arrival of twenty years work and a re-statement, now perfectly conscious, of various themes which were to be further developed in their profoundest dimensions in the works which followed. The interpretation of life in its many different aspects, which Moravia offers here, becomes a historical representation of a society with wider horizons than that of his usual middle class. And perhaps there is no book which reveals so well the contribution to the Fascist dictatorship made by the participation and bored indifference of the Italian people—from the highest officials down to the man in the street—just as later *Two*

Women is undoubtedly the most beautiful and accurate novel about the War written in Italy. This first broad canvas of a large segment of Italian society is still drawn in terms of the psychological story of Adriana, Mino, and the other characters. Nevertheless, it is clear that the restored freedom of speech has already borne fruit. In *The Woman of Rome*, Moravia's work enters a new dimension. He is no longer concerned with presenting a *bourgeoisie* in decay, or problems of sex solely from the inside, as he had done hitherto; a vein of frank social polemic dispels the atmosphere of stagnation that had pervaded some of his earlier novels.

The story of Adriana is that of an ordinary, rather naïve girl who, driven on by her mother, a woman worn out by life, possessed solely by a bitter desire for revenge, becomes the slave of her own ingenuousness and inclinations. After various unsuccessful attempts to come to terms with life (through art and marriage), she finally becomes a prostitute. Besides Gino, who has seduced her with a false promise of marriage, the people who influence her life are Mino, a student who does not reciprocate her love, Astarita, a Fascist ruffian who is overwhelmed by a dark, fierce, hopeless passion for her, and Sonzogno, a crazy murderer, tormented by his own violence, by whom Adriana conceives a child. The novel closes with Mino's suicide, which Moravia intends as a seal on the alienation of another intellectual, and with the death of Astarita at the hands of Sonzogno who, in his turn, is killed by the police. Here are three examples of fated men, each in his own way full of a certain inhuman fascination, which is contrasted with the sweetness and "purity" of Adriana and her capacity for hope and renunciation, even when confronted by the harshest trials of life.

Expressed in the abstract terms of a summary, the story of *The Woman of Rome* may seem absurd. Three violent deaths at the end of the novel, rather along the

lines of the detective story, seem to be the penalty
which Moravia paid in his search for a wider public.
And this may be true in part, for undoubtedly in *The
Woman of Rome* even the least discerning of readers can
find something to suit his taste. The lives of all the
characters are closely interwoven, especially in the
second half of the novel. Here the reader's pleasure in
the story for its own sake is exploited according to the
nineteenth-century formula, with foreshortenings, cuts
and opportune resumptions in the narrative. Referring
specifically to Defoe's *Moll Flanders*, which apparently
had first suggested the idea of the book to him,
Moravia made clear in an article[1] the reasons which had
allowed him to adopt its plot technique in a modern
spirit, as an almost surrealistic device, without pretending
to naturalistic fidelity in the depiction of events. He con-
cluded by observing that "anyhow no one would claim
that the 'natural' deaths of the naturalistic writers do
not belong in their turn to a convention, even if of
another type." But the same article also contains statements which were to spark off the polemics on *The
Woman of Rome*. Above all, in referring to his intentions,
Moravia indicated in a particular passage what once
used to be called in Italy "the moral" of the book, that
is, its nucleus. In it Adriana is still at the beginning of
her life as a prostitute. In an all out attempt to change
her way of life, she is tortured by doubts for half a day,
but, weighed down by her own temperament and stark
reality, she gives up the struggle forever:

So, after a few hours of anguish, I gave up the unequal
struggle against what appeared my fate, indeed, I
welcomed it with more affection, as one embraces a
foe one cannot defeat, and I felt liberated. Some may
think it far easier to accept an unworthy but profit-
able fate than to renounce it. But I have often wondered why misery and anger dwell in the hearts of those

people who try to live according to certain precepts and to conform to certain ideals, and why those who accept their destiny—which is mainly emptiness, obscurity and feebleness—are often so gay and carefree. In such cases, the individual does not follow a precept but his own temperament, which appears to him in the guise of a real destiny. My temperament, as I have already said, was to be gay, amiable and serene, at all costs, and I accepted it.[2]

It is immediately clear that we are once again at the core of Moravia's existentialist writing, which opens out here into a perspective not present in *The Time of Indifference* and poses at the same time some problems and doubts.

The Time of Indifference, standing as a forerunner of existentialism, a novel which is completely instinctive, spontaneous, and asystematic, was in fact dominated by the dangerous note of absolute negation. Our naked everyday business of living was there exposed in a phase of complete disintegration in which resistance and even hope are radically rejected. It was not, therefore, an existentialism which offered, as in the best examples, a new and clearer view of human slavery and so constituted, ultimately, a salutary operation: but rather, an existentialism still in the sphere of romantic Wagnerian canons, and more like Rimbaud's rebellion and dissolution than the final acceptance of life of Sartre's Ronquentin.

Adriana, the woman of Rome, is also invested with all the qualities characteristic of an existentialist view of the human condition, such as a sense of absurdity and defeat; and yet she reaches a tentative stage where, in spite of everything, she finds the strength to live with some peace of mind in the face of a cruel destiny. The way she is presented is marked by a progression towards greater serenity.

M F

Falconi observes that:

The protagonist of *The Woman of Rome* is a creature whom too many have been unable to resist placing amongst the most celebrated "fallen women" of the sentimental nineteenth century, with its longing for "redemption." Admittedly, the elements which would allow *The Woman of Rome* to be placed in a similar category are infinite in number. Yet to do so would be superficial. *The Woman of Rome* is not at all a Dostoevskian Sonja, nor a posthumous lady of the Camellias: she is rather (though not only and not really—and this is the measure of Moravia's realism—) a mother-goddess of life, whose generous and merciful bosom welcomes whoever has need to forget his solitude and to find faith again: she herself suffers, yet endures, despairing deeply but always calm and trusting, wise and fearless: on the whole an authentic existentialist ideal of womanhood.[3]

Let her supply her own commentary:

I went on being the same Adriana, with the same character who took men home for money and went about with Gisella and talked of unimportant things with my mother and with everyone else. And I thought it was strange that I was so different alone from what I was in company, in my relationship with myself and with other people. But I did not flatter myself that I was the only one to have such violent and desperate feelings. I imagined everyone, at least once a day, must feel his own life reduced to a single point of absurd, ineffable anguish—except that their knowledge produced no visible effect upon them, either. They left their houses as I did, and went around playing sincerely their insincere parts. This thought strengthened me in my belief that all men, without exception, deserve to be pitied, if only because they are alive.[4]

With Adriana, as with Agostino, Moravia is no longer the novelist of a closed world which is evil and condemned to a few destructive feelings. And this new pity in the author is reflected, by this time, in all his characters. From the mother who is imprisoned within her own dramatic silence (at a certain point only her eyes speak for her) to Astarita, the black-shirt ruffian, he too inwardly tormented by a desperate solitude, and by a hopeless passion devoid of all relief ("I curse the day I met you and the day I was born"[5]). And finally Mino, the usual Moravian *bourgeois* intellectual. He too is clinically tainted by dark obsessions, and at once hurled into an atmosphere of tragedy.

Referring to the passage just quoted, in which Adriana reveals her decision to accept life as it is, Moravia went on:

This passage in my opinion should furnish all those who take the trouble to look for it, with the key, not only to *The Woman of Rome*, but also to several of my other books. The relationship between Adriana and the student in *The Woman of Rome* is the one which occurs between those who accept destiny, that is to say, their own temperament and the determining natural and social factors, and those who do not. It is also the relationship between a passive nature—indeed without any doubt, the relationship between *nature* itself—and an active principle. But the same relationship existed already in the now distant *Time of Indifference* of 1929, between Michele and his mother, and his family in general. The corrupt and obtuse placidity, that is, the *nature* of the mother, corresponds to an acute and innocent placidity—that is, the *nature* of Adriana. To the tension of Michele, to his effort of will, of judgment, his longing for action, correspond the tension, the effort, the desire for action and judgment of Mino. Both the mother and Adriana *continue*;

like nature they have no history. Both Michele and
Mino *end*; that is, they finish in a story both human
and abstract. . . . Compared with *The Time of Indifference*, the relationship between nature and the
active principle is modified only in the sense of a
greater richness of nature, no longer seen through
moral spectacles, and of a greater tragedy and in-
flexibility of the active principle, led back to a more
vigorous coherence. The mother is neither so rich nor
so good as Adriana, nor is Michele so desperate and
resolute as Mino.[6]

All this is substantially true. The feeling remains, however, that Mino is overdone, in the way Moravia
indicates. More than a victim of his environment, this
character has all the qualities of a paranoiac. There is
little point in demonstrating Mino's paranoia. The book
speaks for itself. "Loved but not loving, repenting of
actions not yet done, dead before having lived, and in
the end a suicide,"[7] Mino remains in our memory, not
so much as an alienated intellectual, but rather as a
typical pathological case from a psychiatrist's case book.

REFERENCES

1. "Perchè ho scritto *La Romana*," 1947.
2. *W.R.*, p. 201.
3. Falconi, "I vent'anni di
   Moravia," pp. 189-205.
4. *W.R.*, pp. 162-3.
5. *W.R.*, p. 369.
6. "Perchè ho scritto *La Romana*," 1947.
7. Del Buono, *op. cit.*, p. 53.

CHAPTER IX

"THE RULES OF THE GAME"

Mino's lack of vitality, his pathological, total negativism is revealed quite plainly in the character of Luca in *Disobedience* (1948), and in his sterile and paralysing revolt against life. Mino's immobility and his chilling fatalism do not testify to a struggle against a whole culture and society, but merely represent a crisis of spiritual inadequacy, producing a rejection made so absolutely that it spurns any ray of hope or any connexion with the world. Such immobility and fatalism are the ingredients which Moravia adopts for the laboratory experiment or clinical report of *Disobedience*, and then twists and refines so as to give them the appearance of a revolt against society, and finally cures by the unexpected panacea of sex. Sex provides the magic touch which makes Luca, the main character, surrender himself to life, accept and find peace in that "despicable normality" of *bourgeois* society which he feared so much. A neat about-turn from "history" to "nature," contrasting with Agostino and his "all-consuming dream" of an unattainable "innocent land."

"Not feeling himself in harmony with the life around him," observed Falqui[1] "this young man turns against it, repels it, shuns it through a disobedience which becomes a systematic renunciation of every duty and pleasure, affection and desire, until he finally approaches death as 'perhaps the only true pleasure'." In his turn Flora asked[2] "what unspoken wrong" generated that rancour, "that anger which is a key-word in Moravia" and "not only in the story of the adolescent Luca, who reaches anger through the most obscure and futile of motives."

In reality the motives are neither so futile nor so obscure. Moravia speaks clearly, as a passage from the opening pages of the book will suffice to show:

> After spending the summer holiday at the usual sea-side place Luca went back to the town where he lived, feeling that he was not well, and would in fact soon fall ill. . . . He had always gone to school and it seemed natural to him to go on doing so—even if, sometimes, the things that he had to learn appeared to present themselves before him, not arranged in orderly fashion in the future, according to the days and months of the scholastic year, but all heaped up in front of him in a steep, unsurmountable mass, like a mountain whose smooth sides offer a climber no hold for hand and foot. It was not the will which was lacking, but rather some physical impulse, some fortitude of the body which he could not identify. His body sometimes seemed to give way beneath him, like an exhausted horse dull-eyed with fatigue beneath a rider who spurs it vainly on.
>
> Often, however, this body of his rebelled when Luca least expected, not so much in face of heavy risks as for reasons of little or no importance. Luca, at this time, was subject to sudden, furious rages. . . .[3]

In the opening pages, Moravia accumulates all the symptoms of Luca's illness, which will develop along the classical Freudian lines of inverted aggressiveness (anger which transforms itself into disobedience through a form of self-destructive nihilism) up to the point of the liberation of the sexual instinct which impedes the fixation of those impulses and their degeneration into suicide. (It was A. Miotto,[4] in 1949, in a study of the novel from a strictly psychoanalytical point of view, who stressed that Luca's disobedience has schizophrenic tendencies). This is, then, a case-book study in the Freudian manner, on which it may be useful to dwell for a moment to indicate how much Moravia may have sensed what poetry can exist in a clinic. It is enough to point out Moravia's frequent references, to a "dark arid, ungrateful obstinacy," an "iron and abstract logic," an "experimental curiosity," the "rules of the game," the "bitter game of disobedience," an "almost strident adhesion to a comedy of misunderstandings," the "mechanical and exact quality of a game," the development of a "plan." Moravia, records Hauser, "writes without sympathy. The boy Luca comes to life for a moment only, and one is left at the end feeling that, though there are doubtless good reasons for writing the book, there are not very many for reading it."[5] Kemp, in his turn, observes: "Bravo Moravia. But bravissimo when he tells us of other things and other people. About mature things, not larvae."[6] If a shortcoming of a human order does occur, it lies in the author's insistence on depicting the various aspects of sick adolescence. Everything, whether animate or inanimate, constantly appears to be affected by some contagion. This is a "degeneration" of the world and of life, such as to render wholly inadequate even the "historical" explanations of the malady which the author is ready to provide. The novel fails in the case-book dryness of its external structure, and in the narrowness of its approach. Such a shortcoming is only partly counterbalanced by the subtle and vigorous art with which language is used. The diction of this novel does, however, reflect the unfailing consistency of Moravia's gifts as a writer of narrative prose.

If the pathological vices which are denounced with such monotonous insistence by Moravia in *Disobedience*, denounce in their turn the vices of the work itself, its extreme poverty of perspective and meagre range of colouring, Luca's sophisticated distortion and his consequent ambiguity in face of his own society must still be considered.

Here, as we have seen, Moravia has explicitly shown Luca as mentally ill: first in the detailed descriptions at the beginning of the book, and then in a series of actions and thoughts which mirror every facet of his pathological condition. But there is also a kind of dislocation. The book, which began with the air of a psychological essay or a clinical report, ends by claiming to be the more common and more widely significant drama of a typical adolescent who must adapt himself to a society that seems to be compelling him to accept the role it has designed for him.

"He rebelled against a life with which everyone wanted him to compromise. He felt impelled to cut himself off from the things he *hated* precisely because he *loved* them too much: a few objects, money, books: he wanted to break these ties which were also a sign of obedience to the destiny which had been imposed on him without his ever being consulted."[7] Even the fear of punishment at school "seemed to him preferable to the usual automatic obedience. With a punishment, at least, the profoundly coercive nature of life was fully revealed with no more hypocritical pretences."[8] "And so, he reflected nevertheless, if you don't accept what other people want you to be, or believe you to be, you either get punished or you're thought to be ill."[9] And to the teacher who asked him what he was thinking, he would have liked to reply: "I'm learning how not to think."[10] Throughout the novel, both the drama of an illness, and the much wider drama of the alienation of a boy can be witnessed at the same time—which thus brings to light the social and the class element (the immediate violence of surrounding reality), and yet confines it within the restricted perspective of a pathological case. The absolute hostility of the individual towards man and things in a twisted society; the total lack of participation, indeed the open conflict with the world; the "revolt on the part of inanimate objects,"[11] the "incapacity on his own part to love and to dominate them,"[12] all this does not therefore present itself with the force of an objective, communicable truth, because, in *Disobedience*, it is once again the pathological aspect of the situation which predominates, and the more natural social aspect assumes in the end the artificially distorted character of an adaption to a pre-determined situation. Luca's "desire for renunciation, for resignation"[13] does not really constitute a protest or a coherent renunciation of life of one who does not wish to compromise with life through vice or complicity; but, as with Mino in *The Woman of Rome*, and even with Dino in *The Empty Canvas* (who was born bored), springs mainly from a weakness of the mind and nerves, a pathological incapacity for action.

It is no wonder, therefore, that Luca's renunciation, his "continual systematic disobedience to the duties, affections and pleasures which his existence suggest to him and imposes upon him,"[14] are resolved afterwards, quite outside any concrete dimensions of history and society, through the Freudian miracle of sex, which heals everything. In fact sex holds the magnificent offer of an all-soothing compromise, through vice and complicity, with that "despicable normality" of the middle classes which was at first so much feared. Once Moravia has dealt with the illness along Freudian lines, all is cured, and Luca, no longer ill, will not only no longer stand up against the errors of his world, but rather will enjoy them in peace, as a good *bourgeois*:

And he knew that, from now onwards, not only the clatter of a train in a tunnel or the whiteness of snow on a mountain peak, but all things would have a meaning for him and would speak to him in their own mute language. Then the train, with another whistle, came out into the light of day.[15]

REFERENCES

1. Falqui, *Prosatori e narratori del novecento italiano*, 1950, pp. 431-41.
2. Flora, *op. cit.*, pp. 197-231.
3. *T.A.*, p. 87.
4. Miotto, "Moravia e la psicanalisi," 1949.
5. Hauser, in *New Statesman*, 14 Oct. 1950.
6. Kemp, "La vie des livres ... qui nous viennent d'Italie," 1949.
7. Flora, *op. cit.*, pp. 197-231.
8. *T.A.*, p. 161.
9. *T.A.*, p. 164.
10. *T.A.*, p. 99.
11. *T.A.*, p. 88.
12. *Ibid.*
13. *T.A.*, p. 95.
14. Cover flap of the Bompian edn.
15. *T.A.*, p. 200.

CHAPTER X

THE POST-WAR PERIOD

The years in which *Disobedience* was written were difficult
years for Italy, a shattered country newly emerged from
the War and plunged into the chaos and the monopo-
listic speculations of economic recovery. The fall of
Fascism brought with it the destruction of an established
order, however negative, of relationships between the
individual and the world, and it was essential to find a
new set of standards and a rule of law. The previous
solidarity of the Italian resistance crumbled beneath the
inert conservatism of Roman Catholicism and the tena-
cious rancour that recent history had left in the minds
of the masses. Meanwhile at the top of the pyramid the
cold and astute game of political calculation was beginning. Artistic activity, which is always rooted in history,
even when it takes the form of escape, shared the general
need for revival.

Emotions were running high, and there was wide-
spread uneasiness about the cultural achievements of the
past, which seemed to have no bearing on the present
dilemma. Under the Fascist régime the Italian poets
had developed a hermetic poetry in which they sought to
express subjective truths, and had thus entered, in their
way, into the stream of contemporary European literature. They were thus able to strike a blow against senti-
mentality in literature, patriotism, Fascist politics and
rhetoric. But the novelist, as we have already seen, was
in a very different position. The novel is a *genre* which
by definition should be the most open form of dialogue
between the artist and society. Novelists had to some

extent preserved a dignified silence by confining themselves to the absurdly narrow limits of the "prosa d'arte" ("fine writing") and the "bella pagina." But times had changed. They now had to overcome the deadly stagnation of public opinion in Italy, which saw the novel not as a creative work of art with direct implications for mankind, but as a purely literary work, considered external form without troubling too much about the life behind it, and was not seriously concerned to discover whether the novel embodied the contradictory humanity of modern man.

Moravia's *The Time of Indifference*, as we have already seen, with its bitter undisguised tone of accusation, its monotonous, insistent, bitingly essential phrases which seemed almost to bear a note of blunt protest, had, as early as 1929, already shattered the fixed patterns of Italian prose, and thus came to assume the character and the responsibilities of historic significance. But *The Time of Indifference* had remained an isolated example with no following, and in the vast majority of cases it had been read in reverse. Instead of seeing their own reflexion, the Fascist *bourgeoisie* had seen in it the simple story of a familiar intrigue amongst not very respectable people: a fact which had made the circulation of the novel possible. And each of Moravia's succeeding works remained an isolated achievement. This is just as true of the books which powerfully developed the theme of moral responsibility first put forward in *The Time of Indifference* as it is of those which, by their ambiguous and inconclusive results, betrayed this same theme.

But now the times had changed for everyone. The victory of the Allied forces, the Marshall plan, and the rhythmic beat of boogie-woogie violently swung the attention of the European public to America and to what appeared then to be its message of liberalism and peace. The American literary voice seemed to be fresh and invigorating, and the American writers, standing outside the traditions and the overwhelming heritage of centuries of European culture, became very fashionable. Already, at the height of Fascist rule, Pavese and Vittorini, through their massive work as translators, critics and novelists, had fought to introduce into Italy the voice of America. But what for them had been the assiduous and honest pioneering work of grafting on something new—whilst they remained conscious of the lessons of centuries of inimitable tradition—now became not only a fashion, but very soon an illness. Hemingway's interpretation of the world in terms of the wisdom of the virile, experienced adventurer, with its adolescent vigour and limitations, became the mirage they all pursued. Suddenly Moravia seemed outdated. The essayist, the existentialist, the novelist of alienation from life already seemed rooted in the past. A more contingent reality of unemployment and hunger was closing in. Along with the Americans, the Vittorini of *Conversations in Sicily* and the Pavese of *Bitter Harvest* and *The Moon and the Bonfire* became the masters.

However, these books, despite their novelty, did not have any immediate successors. Too many writers, different by nature and education, found themselves thrown together by circumstances, protesting the faith of the moment. And meanwhile ideals and hopes were fading away. Now that the chaotic phase of the early post-war years had passed, the Italian and European *bourgeoisie* began to rot again, showing all the signs of impenitence. It was the age of the great monopolies, the terrible accumulation of armaments continued, and experiments were made in the newest and most fearful techniques of collective destruction. The situation of Italian literature at that time seemed to reflect this state of affairs. Pavese, shaken by a deep lack of faith in man, committed suicide; Vittorini's long silence began; and the first phase of Italian neo-realism threatened to end in futile experimentalism.

Moravia's critical faculty was directed against the American writers. His criticism of their work, from his devastating review of Saroyan to the recent, rather brutal attack on Hemingway's decadence, strikes home. With complete independence of judgment, the author of *The Time of Indifference* and of the realistic pages of *The Woman of Rome*, worked obstinately, published in isolation, freely followed his own inclination, even at the cost of accumulating pages of dead writing. At a time when Italian writers were making open declarations of the need to express social reality, Moravia seemed to stand apart. *Conjugal Love* was published in 1949, in a volume with some short stories, *The Conformist* in 1951. *The Conformist* is a failure, the greatest disappointment in Moravia's work since the far-off *Ambizioni Sbagliate* of 1935. *Conjugal Love* is a work of almost pompous banality. The curve of Moravia's creativity seemed to have ended in tired repetition and the critics were wondering why he did not resign himself to abandoning the field of creative writing.

Conjugal Love, in reality not a short story but a short novel, is a novel of the eternal triangle. The three characters are the husband, an aspiring writer; his malignantly sensual wife, Leda; and her lover, a lascivious Sicilian barber. The husband, Silvio Baldeschi, is writing a novel, and loses himself in dreams of literary glory, while his wife becomes fascinated with the barber. But Baldeschi's book turns out to be a failure, and the novel ends with a reconciliation between husband and wife.

Silvio Baldeschi is also an existentialist character, "a man tormented by anguish, and always on the border of despair."[1] However, his character is sketched in a somewhat summary fashion, while the figure of Leda is portrayed no less abstractly and casually. Moravia does not exploit the opportunity of exploring an existentialist puzzle, closely set against the background of a society.

The description of the vortex of anguish, the hopes of a woman's love and of artistic creation, the meeting with Leda, infidelity, the reconciliation, are thus situated in a kind of historical void, and not really inside history, and *Conjugal Love* appears as a lost opportunity which will only subsequently be fulfilled in *A Ghost at Noon*, a fine novel. But Baldeschi's final acceptation of life, his attempt to escape from anguish through art, understood in the classical sense of consolation, appear once again, through the problematical debasing of "history" to "nature," far less convincing than the "all-consuming dream" of Agostino. If the natural regression from "history" to "nature" was acceptable (in the sense of a bitter, calm resignation) for Adriana, an uneducated and ingenuous woman of the people, it is certainly far less satisfactory for an intellectual like Silvio Baldeschi.

Far more successful are the short stories published with *Conjugal Love*. "Back to the Sea,"[2] "The Negro and the Old Man with the Bill-hook"[3] and "Contact with the Working Class"[4] are distinguished by their perfect construction and the maturity of their conception. In them all the themes of Moravia's best work are well blended, moving, and full of promise.

The tight circle which encloses the black universe of the worst of Moravia's writing, appears, on the other hand, even more confined in *The Conformist*. The desperate search for normality and conformity by the Fascist Marcello "his desire to adhere to a recognised and general order of things; a wish to be like all the others, since to be different meant to be guilty" seems absurd, and is frustrated by the incredible somersaults and acrobatics of the plot, which is here truly a law unto itself. The vividness of the relationship between Marcello and the society around him is once more needlessly distorted and nullified by morbid elements (the protagonist's tendency to homosexuality and crime) which mingle with existentialist features (the first part of the novel recalls Sartre's *Enfance d'un Chef*). There remains only the dry graphic power of the style which, even here, gives tone and volume to a great many pages and can also make the book, full as it is of facts, characters, and suspense, and closely organised to cover a period of over thirty years, a fascinating work of "literature." It is also a good representation of the sense of solitude and of black suffocating anguish that were part of life under the Fascist dictatorship.

REFERENCES

1. *C.L.*, p. 13.
2. In *Bitter Honeymoon*, 1954.
3. In *The Wayward Life and Other Stories*, 1960.
4. *Op. cit.*

CHAPTER XI

ROMAN TALES AND A GHOST AT NOON

If Moravia's course as a novelist after *The Conformist* no longer has the rhythm it once had, Moravia has nonetheless not abandoned his role of interpreter. Always alive to literary and social matters he speculates in other ways on reality: he travels, writes criticism, discusses, polemicises, never ceases to meditate on the cultural implications of current events.

In 1952, the best short stories published by the author since the beginning of his career came out in one thick volume. It was possible now, in the face of the freshness and novelty of his earlier writing to observe more clearly the tiredness of his later production which, since *The Woman of Rome*, seemed to have added nothing to the sum of anguish and searching contained in that book, an anguish and a searching begun thirty years ago in *The Time of Indifference*. But it was just at that time, when the circle seemed finally closed, that the *Corriere della Sera* regularly featured some short stories witten in the first person, in which characters stepped forward for a moment to talk about themselves and disappeared once more when their adventure (or rather their misadventure) was over.

These short stories all present more or less the same structure. "The openings," says Limentani:

are vigorous and reveal a writer of real power: he introduces the character of the narrator in dense and clear syntheses, now through the *chiaroscuro* of contrast with another person, now through the memory of a past episode; then, with an *enough* or an *in short*, we enter into the real story, which thus almost takes on the value of a demonstration and a proof of the initial premisses; in the end, in one way or another, the narrator pays the price of an adventure in which he has imprudently involved himself or into which others have succeeded in dragging him: and nothing remains for him but to draw from his own bad luck the moral for the others, confirming what was said at the beginning.[1]

The stories continued to appear with bureaucratic punctuality for a couple of years, and in 1954, when the first series of 61 was published in volume under the title *Roman Tales*, it became clear that they were not only valid as individual short stories, but that, taken together, they formed a body of work presenting a well defined panorama of the Roman *petite bourgeoisie*, proletariat, and sub-proletariat.

"I think," explains Moravia:

that the limits of the newspaper columns have been useful to me: no less than the limits, let us say, of the sonnet were useful in its time to the poets who adopted it. This narrow limit suggested to me a form of highly concentrated narration, rapid and direct. To obtain these effects and that technique, I made use of the spoken language in the first person, rather as Belli did in his sonnets in the Roman dialect. The first person allows a rather different tempo from that of the objective third person, more rapid, more synthetic, more, let us put it this way, conventional. This first person then, is almost always that of a man of the people or of the *petite bourgeoisie*. . . . Through the character who says "I", I have in fact tried to make Rome speak, or rather certain groups and parts of the Roman people.[2]

With the same cold, critical detachment with which he

had observed the middle class, Moravia now looks at this new, plebeian and disinherited Rome of people who live by various trades, or more often by illegal rackets; the Rome of the slums, the bars of the drab suburban cafés and of the prostitutes; a Rome of lorry drivers, porters, tinkers, butchers, mechanics, always the prey of their own, everyday misfortune—exclusively economic beings. "They are the Marxist archetypes, in that their first concern is their belly"[3]: for them "non-material values do not seem to have the right to exist and the moral conscience is hardened to the extent that men, moved only by appetite, seem more and more to resemble automatons."[4] The fundamental fact for these characters is the struggle for survival: they must eat or die. Hard and unfeeling in a life of trickery, deception, and dishonesty, they scarcely remain above the level of a violent break with the law, and exist in the constant dimension of the resigned fatalism of "getting by": the typical "I'm all right Jack" of the Roman masses:

When that good lady who came to bring help from the Roman Soccorso asked, she too, why we brought so many children into the world, my wife, who was down in the dumps that day, told her the truth: "If we had money, we would go to the pictures, in the evening . . . but since we haven't we go to bed, and so the children are born." The lady on hearing this was very taken aback and went away without opening her mouth. And I played hell with my wife because it is not always a good idea to tell the truth; and before you do, you've got to know who you are dealing with.[5]

Although the centre of interest for the writer in these new characters is, as in *The Woman of Rome*, substantially of a psychological nature, it is not difficult to show that Moravia has taken a further step towards social inspiration of a more objective kind. The socio-economic factor in life is here quite explicitly stated in an utterly unmannered portrayal of the reality of the Roman proletariat. Clearly resuming the discourse interrupted at the time of *The Woman of Rome*, Moravia was now moving decisively towards the great fresco of *Two Women*. Here too, of course, his strong individuality tends to distort this new reality into the usual "Moravian" dimension, to lay bare, in the cross beams of sexuality and an implacable moralism, the most unpleasant and repellent aspects of his characters, often reducing them to the dimensions of a comic or grotesque game. But substantially, as Limentani again observes:

the writer has in the meantime emerged from his chrysalis, has left behind the closed *bourgeois* world and has directed an ever more encompassing gaze on the men round about him: the popular world is that which has attracted him most and held his attention; he invests it always with his own overwhelming subjectivity but finds in that reality a firm resistance to his permanent tendency to a disfiguring violence.[6]

It is also possible to trace in these stories the line of a definite literary tradition, from the naturalistic stories of Verga to Belli's poetic sketches about Roman life, and finally, perhaps, to occasional echoes from American writing. But the native originality of the writer is such that to lay too much stress on these antecedents would give a misleading account of his remarkable achievements.

However, before *Two Women*, Moravia returned to the triangular situation he had used so unhappily in *Conjugal Love*. In *A Ghost at Noon* published at the end of the same year, 1954, he applies this situation to the relationship between the conscience of the intellectual and reality.

Emilia and Riccardo Molteni, a writer by vocation and a script-writer by necessity, fall in love, marry and form a perfect couple. But suddenly, for no apparent reason, this relationship falls apart. It simply will not work. Molteni fails both to bridge the abyss which has opened between them or to find the cause of it. His wife no longer loves him but despises him. The novel ends with Emilia's death in a car accident while running away with Battista, a film producer. But Riccardo will go on dreaming about her in the way he always has, trying in vain to understand what has happened.

I went back, then, and lay down again in the deck-chair, and with a trembling hand lit a cigarette. It seemed to me, however, that whether I was despicable or not—and I was convinced that I was not—I still retained my intelligence, a quality which even Emilia recognised in me and which was my whole pride and justification. I was bound to think, whatever the object of my thought might be; it was my duty to exercise my intelligence fearlessly in the presence of any kind of mystery. If I abandoned the exercise of my intelligence, there was indeed nothing left to me but the disheartening sense of my supposed, but un-proved, despicableness.

And so I started to think again, in a manner both determined and lucid. In what could it consist, this despicableness of mine?[7]

In giving his verdict against A Ghost at Noon, Jean Pouillon wrote[8] in 1955: "Everything is said perfectly, but nothing is really understood. The limpidity of the narrative persists despite the obscurity of its significance, and what ought to appear behind the highly polished window pane of the language remains finally uncertain. As for the reader," he continues, referring to the main characters, "he learns nothing but their failure."

In reality Pouillon's whole article could be read in reverse, since the critic has not taken into account the fact that many of what he considers failings constituted, historically, the extreme vitality of the novel; indeed, this is possibly Moravia's most conscious effort so far in his long study of the relationship between the intellectual and *bourgeois* society. Here, too, as in previous works and as later in *The Empty Canvas*, this study is worked out in the simpler and clearer psychological terms of the relationship between an intellectual and a woman; the woman, in her "naturalness," that is in her complete adaptation to the society about her, with which she is perfectly at one, and which she therefore represents and mirrors, is taken directly as a symbol for "reality." And thus it would be false to debase everything in the terms used by Fernandez when he observes that *A Ghost at Noon* deals with sexual disgust, and that Emilia is silent in front of the attempts of Riccardo to find a reason for their failure, simply because she realises that all words and analysis would be vain and derisory beside the intense reality of the sexual act: "Riccardo tries ceaselessly to draw Emilia into the world of ideas and sentiments; Emilia brings him back ceaselessly to the brutal reality of indubitable facts, which existed before language itself."[9]

"The brutal reality of indubitable facts" is something very different from what Fernandez suggests.

This is seen immediately:

"But why d'you despise me?"

"Because I do," she cried all at once; "because you're made like that, and however hard you try, you can't change yourself."

"But how am I made?"

"I don't know how you're made—*you* ought to know ... I only know you're not a man, you don't behave like a man."[10]

Here, to be a man, to be made like a man, does not mean to know how to make love, for Emilia never throws any doubt on Riccardo's virility: it means, in accordance with the scale of *bourgeois* values which Emilia embodies, and which she faithfully represents, to be like Battista, a vulgar *nouveau riche* film producer, a speculator and counterfeiter of culture. The background brings the novel into sharp historical perspective through the various characters of the Roman film world, with which Moravia himself was at that time in contact as script-writer for his own stories and novels: a world of base interests, dominated by the German Rheingold, the director for whom Molteni was to write a script based on the *Odyssey* and, of course, the producer and speculator Battista, with his villa in Capri. Quite naturally, Molteni's rationalism and intellectual honesty, already undermined by compromise with the cinema, founder in this degenerate world. Battista wants to make a money-spinning epic; Rheingold, a sham intellectual with a superficial knowledge of Freud (he has no sense of *bourgeois* degeneration, and is wholly integrated in it) wants a psychological film, and Molteni wants to re-create the enchanted atmosphere of Homer's poetry:

... "but I myself am convinced that, even to-day, the *Odyssey* could be made as Homer wrote it. . . ."

"That's an aspiration on your part, Molteni. . . . You aspire after a world like that of Homer . . . you would like it to be so . . . but unfortunately it isn't."

I said conciliatingly: "Let's leave it at that, then: I aspire after that sort of world. . . . You, on the other hand, do not!"[11]

This is a powerless aspiration (and this longing for a barbaric age, as Rheingold does not fail to remark, is also disconcerting), as Molteni himself comes to realise when, to give weight to his idea, he recites the episode of Ulysses in Dante's *Inferno*.

But at the line: "*O frati, dissi che per cento milia . . .*" I felt my voice, in spite of myself, was trembling with

sudden emotion. I considered how there was contained in those few lines, not merely the idea I had
formed of the figure of Ulysses, but also that of myself and of my life as it ought to have been and, alas,
was not; and I realised that my emotion arose from
the clarity and beauty of this idea in comparison
with my own actual powerlessness.[12]

Here, it is obvious that Molteni follows the model of
Michele and Agostino, rather than that of Mino and
Luca, who were pathological; but he is more fully developed, with an organic power which Moravia had
not achieved before. He too is an intellectual, alienated
in his "all consuming dream," and, precisely because of
the spiritual nobility of that dream, destined to failure
in every concrete experience of life. And destined, therefore, to lose Emilia.

Emilia despises him, as he himself says, "on the basis
of a miserable commonplace,"[13] Emilia "does not live
in an ideal world, but rather in the perfectly real world
of the people like Battista and Rheingold":[14]

And, in order to have the Emilia I loved and to make
her judge me for what I was, I should have had to
carry her away from the world in which she lived
and introduce her into a world as simple as herself,
as genuine as herself, a world in which money did
not count and in which language had retained its
integrity, a world—as Rheingold had pointed out to
me—to which I could aspire, certainly, but which did
not in fact exist.[15]

A world then, where Emilia with all her simplicity and
genuineness, sincere in everything but hopelessly powerless at the level of solid reality, would not be able to
conceive the idea that Riccardo wanted to make use of
her body to secure the friendship of the producer
Battista. That idea automatically degrades even Mora-

via's great reality of sex to the level of a commercial instrument in the hard economic context of Riccardo's and Emilia's *bourgeois* life. It is true to say, but in a sense very different from that intended by Pouillon, that through this degradation, "the reader learns nothing but their failure."[16]

Molteni cannot avoid failure if he remains true to his intellectual principles. Emilia is not all he loses. His involved psychological digressions and his obsessive preoccupation with the snares of dialectic have no power over a reality unaffected by words; but they have the power to make him look like the cloying Ulysses which Rheingold's viscous interpretation demands. Riccardo, like Michele, Agostino, and even Marcello of *The Conformist*, cannot depart from the role which *bourgeois* history forces him to play. But he maintains his intellectual honesty, and at the end of the novel he too is offered a vision of unattainable purity.

After the funeral, in the evening, I closed the door behind me as I entered our apartment—for ever useless and empty now—and I understood at last that Emilia, truly, was dead, and that I should never see her again. All the windows in the flat had been opened wide in the hope of increasing even the faintest breath of air, but I felt I was suffocating nevertheless as I wandered from one room to another, over the polished floors, in the twilight gloom. Meanwhile, the brightly lit windows of the adjoining houses, their inhabitants visible inside the rooms, drove me almost to frenzy, their quiet lights reminding me of a world in which people loved without misunderstandings and were loved in return and lived peaceful lives—a world from which it seemed to me that I was forever shut out.[17]

Once again this is a conflict between history and a dream outside history. We have seen in the proletariat of *Agostino*, *The Woman of Rome*, and *Roman Tales* that they are not really the "quiet lights" of "a world in which people loved without misunderstandings, were loved in return and lived peaceful lives." This is what, to his own cost, Agostino had already learnt, and what Moravia's last hero of alienation, Dino in *The Empty Canvas*, will come to know very well.

REFERENCES

1. Limentani, *op. cit.*, p. 70.
2. Bocelli, "Moravia romano," 1959.
3. "Writers at Work," 1962, p. 201.
4. Bocelli, *op. cit.*
5. "Il pupo," in *Racconti Romani*, p. 97.
6. Limentani, *op. cit.*, p. 60.
7. *G.N.*, pp. 188-9.
8. Pouillon, "Le Mépris," 1950, pp. 757-9.
9. Fernandez, *op. cit.*
10. *G.N.*, pp. 180-1.
11. *G.N.*, pp. 172-3.
12. *G.N.*, p. 173.
13. *G.N.*, p. 191.
14. *Ibid.*
15. *Ibid.*
16. Pouillon, *op. cit.*
17. *G.N.*, p. 205.

CHAPTER XII

TWO WOMEN

Roman Tales had been characterised by a kind of literary obstinacy. Through a portrait gallery of events and characters, the stories brought working-class Rome to life: but Moravia's imperturbable objectivity gave them the somewhat abstract quality of a social enquiry. However, the publication of *Two Women*, in 1957, marked the great rebirth of the writer.

"After *A Ghost at Noon*," observes Moravia, "I no longer knew what to write. I came across those pages written down after my return to Rome, those on my stay in Ciociaria during the War. I began to sketch out a continuation."[1] Meanwhile three years had passed, which Moravia had by no means wasted, being constantly active in the cultural sphere as a critic, speaker, and voracious reader. He firmly resisted the attacks of the aesthetic critics and the Vatican censure (which in 1952 imposed a ban on all his books), and tried to reconfirm, with a conclusive work, his vitality as a novelist, which had recently been shown in *Roman Tales* and *A Ghost at Noon*. If the somewhat summary characterisation, the near caricature of the setting, had prevented *A Ghost at Noon* from attaining the level of *The Time of Indifference*, *Agostino* and *The Woman of Rome*, his new novel, *Two Women*, the profound and highly compassionate expression of a tragic period in the history of a people, marks a memorable date.

Like Adriana in *The Woman of Rome*, Cesira, the woman of the people from Ciociaria, is here a narrator in the first person. Along with her daughter Rosetta, she

abandons her shop in Rome to escape from the bombing
and seeks refuge in her native Ciociaria. But instead of
finding peace, she finds the horror of war. Among the
evacuees in the village, for whom only three things
matter, money, food, and women, Cesira finds Michele.
This new Moravian intellectual will help Cesira to
become aware of many fundamental realities lying just
below the surface of everyday life.

Michele ✗

Michele (and perhaps the name is not without significance) is, first of all, the true anti-Michele of *The
Time of Indifference* and, in general, of the other Moravian
intellectuals. He is intended to represent the idealistic
intellectual who still believes in an exact relation
between facts and words, and who thus accepts the
stress and strain of moral responsibility and does not
resign himself, as Moravia's earlier intellectuals did, to
a frustrating destiny of boredom and passive acceptance.
Michele is able to avoid the inner discord, the internal
contradiction, in short the alienation of those intellectuals
who, conditioned as they are by their society, nevertheless seek to live according to an "active" and coherent
principle. Or better, inner discord and internal contradiction are the source of Michele's strength and will to
fight openly against stolid guilt and hypocrisy. The
contradictions which tear the *bourgeois* world are no
longer acted out in the conscience of the character, but
are indicated in the objectivity of things and people.

Let us look, for example, at Cesira, Michele, and his
father, Filippo, here seen among the evacuees:

> ... as soon as he knew that I had a shop in Rome,
> Filippo immediately became cordial not to say
> brotherly, and, after asking me whether I had money,
> and learning that I had, confided to me that he also
> had a large sum in his trouser pocket, which would
> suffice even if—supposing it to be possible—the
> English delayed their coming for a whole year. He

spoke to me in a confidential tone, as between equals,
as between one shopkeeper and another, in fact: and
again I felt reassured. . . . Filippo said, further: "We
are staying up here until the English come, and we're
going to eat and drink and not worry about anything.
. . . When the English arrive, they'll bring wine and
oil and flour and beans and there'll be plenty of everything and we shopkeepers will start up our businesses
again as though nothing had happened." I objected
—if only in order to say something—that there was a
possibility that the English would not come at all
and that the Germans would win the war. "Well,
what does that matter to us?" he asked, "Germans or
English it's all the same thing, provided one of them
wins decisively. All that matters to us is business."
He spoke these words in a loud voice, with great
assurance; and his son who was standing all alone at
the edge of the terrace, looking at the panorama of
the Fondi valley, twisted round like a viper and said,
"It might not matter to you . . . but if the Germans
win I shall kill myself."[2]

This is typical of the relationship between this new
intellectual, and the peasants and petty *bourgeois* world
which surrounds him. As a better illustration of that
relationship and of Michele's consistency within the
dimensions we have just seen, here is the passage in
Chapter IV in which Michele reads aloud one evening
the Bible story of the resurrection of Lazarus. He immediately notices, by obvious signs of boredom, the total
incomprehension and indifference of the evacuees.
"They had, in fact, expected a nice love story," comments
Cesira:

instead of which Michele was reading them the story
of a miracle in which, into the bargain—at least as
far as I could gather—they did not believe any more
than Michele himself believed. . . . The difference I

say, was that Michele, for his part, appeared as he
read to be truly moved by this miracle in which he
did not believe. In fact, when he came to the sentence:
"*And Jesus said, I am the resurrection and the life*", he
broke off for a moment, and we could see that he
had done so because he could not go on owing to the
fact that he was crying. I realised he was crying because of what he was reading and because, as became
clear later, it was related to our present situation. . . .[3]

And then:

I shan't read to you any more because you people
don't understand, and it's no use trying to make
people understand. But remember this, now: each
one of you is Lazarus, and in speaking of Lazarus I
was speaking of you, all of you. Of you, Paride, of
you, Luisa, of you Cesira, of you Rosetta and of myself too, and of my father and of that scoundrel of
Il Tonto and of Severino with his cloth and of the
evacuees up here and of the Germans and the Fascists
down in the valley, and of everybody in fact. You are
all dead, we are all dead and we think we are alive.
As long as we think we are alive because we have our
possessions, our fears, our trifling affairs, our families,
our children, we shall be dead . . . Only on the day
when we realise we are dead, utterly dead, putrified,
decomposed, that we stink of corruption from a mile
away, only then we shall begin to be just barely
alive. . . .[4]

Michele is thus "a young man who sees clearly into
the vicissitudes of his country and of his people . . . to
some extent he is the conscience of Cesira, a precise
point of reference for her lively but amorphous intelligence."[5] Moravia has made us live here through
"the phases in the formation of a conscience: by means
of the Homeric atmosphere of the village based on

family economics, which redeems the shopkeeper from her petty bourgeois rapacity; through the contacts with the intellectual, the German etc. . . . which reveal to her gradually the significance of war; through the good offices of the Moroccans (towards the end Rosetta is raped by Moroccan soldiers) which plunge her once more into incomprehension, but by making her drain the cup of bitterness to the dregs, finally ratify the victory of conscience. . . ."[6] By the end of the novel Cesira and her daughter have become a thief and a prostitute respectively. It is their experience of sorrow, and their acceptance of it, that brings them redemption.

But there is much more in *Two Women* than "phases in the formation of a conscience."[7] Already in 1957, Bocelli spoke of a Moravia who is, "more than ever before, open to certain ranges of sensibility and sentiment, and increasingly determined to proceed from the symbol or the type (still dominant, for example in *Roman Tales*, where the comic and the satiric moods prevail) to the character, and from the depiction of environment and manners to the portrayal of a whole epoch."[8] And, because of the emphasis which Michele always places on purification one suddenly becomes aware in this novel, even more than in *Woman of Rome*, of a sense of total engagement. Technically, it was of some value to Moravia that he was forced to accept a given sequence of facts, which prevented the narrative machine from breaking out (beyond even the limits of the non-naturalistic novel) in the direction of the detective story. The facts of the War were there, and there was no escape from them. The characters are, therefore, represented from the beginning within these predetermined events, which seem calculated to help them come alive and at the same time to let loose the most elemental vitality, by giving free play to the narrator's imagination. Cesira, Rosetta and Michele are seen against the background of wartime Italy, terrified, humiliated, instinctive, rapacious and sentimental, full-blooded and human. The book is written in a dense and smoothly-blended language in which even the landscape is incorporated in the history of the characters and bears witness to their development from instinct and bloodshed to sorrow and compassion.

The writer's thought has evolved from a substantially existentialist phase to a wider social viewpoint, which now allows a stronger emotion in the face of a particular, tragic, experienced reality. It is natural that in the course of this evolution it should become more advantageous for Moravia to employ the first person, the historical necessity of which has been constantly maintained by the author in theory and in practice (except in *The Conformist* and *Disobedience*) since the period of *The Woman of Rome*. "The first person," writes Moravia

is peculiar to present-day narrative. Here it is a question of a first person which is really a first person, and is there to indicate a lack of faith, common to the writer and the reader, in an objective reality, whereas, the third person would denote the existence of such a faith. The omniscience of the nineteenth-century writer had finally resulted in a trick, in a convention empty of life. To-day we can no longer write: "he thought," because we cannot know with certainty what a third person thinks, since there is no longer a thought or a mode of thinking common to all men, we can write only: "I thought."[9]

But, in *Two Women*, it is no longer a question of simply imposing a style on a character, as in *The Woman of Rome*, so that that character, Adriana, can then give expression to her states of mind and her embryonic thoughts, as Moravia himself claims.[10] Here, in the vortex of the War, which reduced everybody's relationship with reality to almost primordial dimensions, Moravia has found a measure of understanding and an elementary

relation with the world. For a moment, the existential
problems of "identity," "relation," and "communication" have been overcome in the common, chaotic
elementarity of a world which once more demands
action. And thus, to this new Moravian Michele, sunk
in a tragically abnormal and terrifying dimension of
reality, indifference and the "dream" are no longer
granted. But this is not all. Because Moravia's interest
in Adriana was mainly of a psychological order, the
narrative "I" of Adriana was often involved in complex
cerebral efforts inappropriate to her character. Here the
narrative "I" is reduced to appropriate and acceptable
terms for the further reason that

> in *Two Women* the interest has shifted from the charac-
> ters to a social reality; and the characters, while
> remaining lively and excellently drawn, serve in the
> first place as an 'observatory': indeed they are that
> social reality, which speaks in the first person through
> one of the individuals of which it is composed.[11]

From this point of view, it is mistaken to exaggerate the
affinity of Cesira with the characters of *Roman Tales*.
Cesira is, it is true, a woman of the people and speaks
with the sententious, bitter, swift and cutting tones of
the various bar-tenders, drivers, tinkers etc., that we
have seen in the *Tales*: but in reality, the little everyday
ups and downs of these stories, their "picturesqueness,"
are here sublimated into a complex story, with an incredible internal tension, in which Cesira is truly the
expression and the symbol of the Italian people, caught
up in the vortex of events more overwhelmingly tragic
than those of the *Roman Tales*.

There is, towards the end of the book, too obvious a
straining for effect, which all the critics have indicated:
that of the unexpected, incredible, or unlikely meta-
morphosis of Rosetta, which caused Cecchi to remark:

M H

Quite naturally, just as one would expect, who should come pounding on to the scene but the Moroccans—complete with burnouses? And they pay her their primitive homage. Till then, that is until the last part of the book, Rosetta had been a beautiful and good girl, a mother's darling, and perhaps, to tell the truth, a little bit of a "cold fish." The violence she suffers suddenly transforms her character. Rosetta loses her inhibitions. . . .[12]

The lack of verisimilitude lies not in the Moroccans' act of violence, nor yet in the unbridled reaction of Rosetta (who for a time becomes a frenzied wanton) but in the fact that that reaction, though it might be true in life, does not here reach truth on the level of art. The last part of the novel thus becomes tumultuous, strained, novelettish, and contorted, in striking contrast with the calm, chaste linearity of the previous two hundred pages. But even so, the final judgment remains the same. And *Two Women*, with its tone of pity, "is likely to remain in our imagination as the strongest and most authentic novel which the war inspired in any of our writers. One of those books which, in all probability, will be discussed for many a day."[13]

REFERENCES

1. Del Buono, *op. cit.*, p. 63.
2. *T.W.*, p. 75-76.
3. *T.W.*, p. 136.
4. *T.W.*, p. 137.
5. Del Buono, *op. cit.*
6. Cases, Answer to "8 domande sulla critica letteraria in Italia," 1960.
7. *Op. cit.*
8. Bocelli, "La Ciociara," 1957.
9. Del Buono, *op. cit.*, p. 51.
10. Preface to *W.R.*
11. Limentani, *op. cit.*, p. 75.
12. Cecchi, "Racconti Romani, Il disprèzzo, La Ciociara," 1958, pp. 169-74 and 264-9.
13. Spagnoletti, "A.M.," 1957, pp. 89-95.

CHAPTER XIII

THE NEO-CAPITALIST MIDDLE-CLASS SOCIETY

While it had seemed that Moravia had found some sense of a relationship among men in re-creating for us the tragically abnormal and terrifying dimension of war, the publication of *The Empty Canvas*, in 1960, was suddenly to reveal *Two Women* as an unrepeatable venture. Indeed, *The Empty Canvas*, his latest long story about the crisis of an intellectual, once more re-opens the existentialist problems of "identity," of "communication," and of the loss of a sense of reality, which, from the very beginning, had formed the anti-*bourgeois* climate of Moravia's narrative.

But if the sense of a life in common, of some warmth in the relationships, however tragic, in our brief span of life, is opened and closed again with *Two Women*, in *The Empty Canvas* the "economic dimension" of existence is definitively held. And if *Two Women* portrayed the reality of war, *The Empty Canvas* aspires to represent the reality of the post-war years, with the logical passage from the portrayal of the Fascist *bourgeoisie* of 1929 and after, to that of the Italian neo-capitalist *bourgeoisie* of the atomic age.

Moravia had great hopes of *The Empty Canvas* which he regarded as much his most important work during the three years which followed the appearance of *Two Women*. In 1958, as witness to his untiring activity, three other books were published: *Un Mese in Russia* (*A Month in USSR*), *Teatro*, and *Nuovi Racconti Romani* (*New Roman Tales*). In *A Month in USSR*, and again in the book published in 1962, *Un' Idea dell' India* (*An Idea of India*), another interesting aspect of Moravia's wide-ranging activity emerges. After Moravia the novelist, the short-story writer, the essayist, the literary critic and film critic, we see here Moravia the traveller. In fact, the two books represent only a part of the series of articles which he had been writing during his travels in Japan, in the United States, and in Egypt, and which were published in the *Corriere della Sera*. More recently the paper has published his articles on black Africa. With the skill needed to catch the most significant aspects of a new and elusive reality, on which he has no time to meditate, Moravia does not lose himself in the artificial colourings so common in this kind of article, but keeps always to the solid facts, remaining true to his usual narrative realism, reporting only what he has seen and heard, without any invention whatever. His opinions on the socio-economic structure and historic evolution of the countries he discusses are less convincing, although they are always stimulating and well organised, and possess that, at times somewhat crude, clarity of ideas which has always been typical of him.

Similarly, the results of his brief flirtation with the theatre are not completely satisfying: these are the adaptation for the theatre of *The Fancy Dress Party*, and the tragedy *Beatrice Cenci*, both published in book-form in 1958. A few years earlier, in collaboration with Luigi Squarzina, Moravia had already adapted *The Time of Indifference* for the theatre.[1] This stage version, which kept entirely to the original structure and preserved a great part of the original dialogue, cannot be considered an independent work of art; it merely underlined the theatrical formation or structure of the novel, which has already been mentioned. The adaptation is skilful, but of course the descriptive passages are omitted, and the monologues which replace the introspective passages are a poor substitute. As a result, the novel's unique tone and much of its fascination are lost.

The *New Roman Tales* are similar to the other *Tales*. The volume contains 69 short stories making 130 in all. Here we have another gallery of independent character sketches, loosely linked by their common background of present-day Rome. Again, the authentic atmosphere of the narrative is created by a few details. The characters and the psychological situations are well drawn, with just as much dramatic movement as is feasible in this type of short story, which, like those of the first collection, had to be printed in the small space of two newspaper columns. On the other hand, it must be said that Moravia, having extracted all he can from these popular situations and characters, now tends to cling to somewhat prefabricated and mechanical situations, in a rather tired and mannered repetition of himself. While his short stories were steadily increasing in number, Moravia recognised that this particular vein was near exhaustion. So he turned instead to drafting a new series. These, too, were first published in the *Corriere della Sera*. Several of them are of rare beauty and faithfully represent the concrete reality of the situations. They appeared in book form at the end of 1962, under the title of one of them, *L'Automa* (*The Fetish*). They are stories of intellectuals, of the *bourgeois*, seen in the new dimension of neo-capitalist middle-class society. "Automatism" is a key word that has appeared more and more frequently in Moravia's work of late: but we may recognise it as simply one of the more obvious aspects of that alienation which has always been a major theme in his work, and which he tackled most systematically and consciously in *The Empty Canvas*.

In an interview[2] granted immediately after the publication of *The Empty Canvas*, Moravia asked his critics not to become engrossed in arguments about his skill as a writer, but instead to concentrate on the contents of the book. In other words, Moravia was inviting the critics to take his descriptive ability for granted and to search for the meaning of the book in the context of contemporary history. Provided that we recognise the author's words as a polemical invitation (a counterblast to aesthetic criticism) to adopt a particular critical orientation, because one can never dissociate form from content in a work of art, it may still be useful to make some general considerations on the neo-capitalist *bourgeois* society which Moravia depicts in *The Empty Canvas* and *The Fetish*.

The society of *The Empty Canvas* is one founded on the idea of purchase and trade. In it even human energy, like everything else which is useful or is accounted such, is changed into something to be bought and sold, which has no value except the value of exchange as determined by supply and demand under existing market conditions. Man himself is thus transformed into something to be bought and sold, and he accepts his life as if it were an investment which must bring him the greatest profit possible under existing market conditions. It follows, then, that when material success (possession) is considered the highest value, relationships between men also follow the same patterns of exchange which control the market of consumer goods and labour. A person's value, therefore, will be proportional to the "resistance" which that person puts up against being "possessed." For example, as soon as one of the partners has been "possessed," or "exploited," a love affair will lose its miraculous nature and will be "extinguished" by mutual antagonisms and disillusionment—in a word by "boredom" (in pathological terms, it will become a symbiosis, an extended egoism of two people "against the rest of the world"). But love should be above all an "attitude," an "orientation of the personality," a desire "to give" and not only "to take," a desire to "love" and not only to be "loved": in other words an "opening" (availability) of the whole soul to the whole of mankind, and then to one person in particular. If this love is not given in our relentless struggle, then human relationships are reduced essentially to those of automatons, alienated from others, from themselves, from nature. And while each one of us tries to be as near as possible to other men by conforming in thought, emotions and behaviour, each one of us remains completely alone, haunted by that deep feeling of uncertainty, anxiety and guilt, which so well reflects the climate of our time.

This is so with the characters in *The Fetish*, and this is what Dino discovers in *The Empty Canvas*, when he finally realises once and for all, that his relationship with Cecilia and with reality in general ("Cecilia that is reality") must end in failure and despair if it is conceived in terms of the *bourgeois* idea of possession.

Dino has a small monthly allowance from his wealthy mother. So as to avoid the boredom which follows material ease, he leaves his mother's country house and retires to an attic in the Via Margutta, in Rome, where he tries to paint. But even there boredom paralyses him to such an extent that one afternoon, considering it useless to attempt escape any longer, he slashes his latest painting with a penknife, while it is still on the easel, and replaces it with an empty canvas to show the definite end of his adventure as an artist and almost of his adventure as a man.

But at this point he meets Cecilia. Wearily, mechanically, this new adventure begins. Cecilia, too, bores him. But, since it is she who first shows definite signs of wishing to leave him (on the very day when he decides to break off the affair), a gloomy jealousy is born in Dino, followed by an ever-increasing desire to possess her: a desire which grows and causes him atrocious suffering, to such an extent that he would now prefer his previous state of apathy, and decides to free himself from Cecilia by analysing what she is, destroying her fascination by means of complete possession. But Cecilia escapes him: she resists all his attempts to explain her and reduce her, in his eyes, to the banality of an everyday thing, of something which has been possessed: money, matrimony. Physical union ever more frequent is not enough. This affair can only finish in the impossibility of continuous physical union, or in death. Dino fails in an attempt to commit suicide, and wakes up in hospital looking at a Lebanon cedar, the symbol of the beginning of understanding: in some place, there must be some "unknown paradise" where he will find a sounder relationship with reality, and therefore also with Cecilia. Up to that time he has only been able to love a Cecilia who refused to give herself to him, that is, a reality which became desirable because it escaped his desire to possess. Now, on the other hand:

I no longer desired to possess her but to watch her live her life, just as she was, that is, to contemplate her in the same way that I contemplated the tree outside my window ... I wondered if possibly, in relinquishing Cecilia, I had also ceased to love her, in other words to experience towards her that same feeling, always delusive and always disappointed, that I had had hitherto, and which, for lack of a more appropriate term, I must call love. I was aware that that kind of love was dead; but that I loved her all the same, though with a love that was new and different. This new love might or might not be accompanied by a physical relationship, but it did not depend upon it, and, in a way, it did not need it. When Cecilia came back we might, or we might not, resume our former relations; but I, in any case, would not cease to love her. . . . And so, in the long run, the only truly certain result was that I had learned to love Cecilia or rather, I had learned to love.[3] Anyhow I hoped I had learned.[4]

In treating a theme as difficult and significant as this, Moravia was taking a decisive step in his career as a novelist. With the refusal to possess, so as not to violate reality, the *bourgeois* Dino chooses the only positive solution accessible to him. It is the price to be paid for one's own moral redemption, and it lies beyond the frustrated impotence of Michele in *The Time of Indifference*, and also beyond Luca's simple withdrawal from history to nature in *Disobedience*. We are confronted here with a historical perception of the world, at a level rarely found in other novelists; which is a further proof of how alive this violently anti-conformist and untiring explorer of crisis has remained, driven by a need to see to the bottom of everything and thoroughly scrutinise every sector of reality.

If we want to make a traditional critical judgment of this rather traditional novel—it remains generally faithful to naturalistic-psychological-objective tradition—it must be said immediately that *The Empty Canvas* is a sketch for a novel, rather than a novel, or, if you like, a novel with a thesis. It is a sketch filled in with events and episodes but without any authentic internal dynamic, shaped and sustained by means of forms which are rather too obvious and worn out. These charges, it should be noticed, are not directed against the style, or against the "representational" aspects of the novel, but against its structure and very "life," which wavers constantly between narrative and essay, without really being either one or the other. The "justification" of the novel lies for the greater part outside the novel itself: in a different, philosophical and therefore more objective standpoint, a standpoint not corrupted and obscured by the actual characters and situations which, as the novel stands, are mere ciphers and artifices.

Yet even in its failure, *The Empty Canvas* shows that Moravia's dossier is still open. Some may maintain that this gnawing of the conscience, the ever repeated clash between a dream of justice and the reality of our historical moment, felt in paroxysmal terms, is absurd. But in reality this is Moravia's unmistakable lesson, as he fixes his gaze on the absurdity of our world, never once straying for a moment into the easy alternative of art conceived as dream or consolation. A writer with ideas, a clearsighted observer and painter of reality who, after overcoming with one blow both D'Annunzio's subjective tradition and the lyricism of "art-prose," refused to be submerged in the monosyllabic rhythms of the post-war Hemingway fashion. At the time he seemed defeated. In fact, in his rejection of all un-restrained technical experimentalism and of art as propaganda, in his loyalty to an ancient and refined tradition of Italian and European culture, and above all in the self-consistency present even in his worst moments—Moravia's achievements now appear valid. In tearing aside the veil of hypocrisy from the preten-sions and the inert self satisfaction of the men responsible for the two Wars, Moravia knew as few others have done how to go straight to the depths of his own ex-periences, to that which Machiavelli called "the effectual truth of the thing" and not "the imagination of it." And there he found the emptiness of the conscience, aliena-tion, the putrid morass in which we are immersed: the bitter experience of men of our time.

REFERENCES

1. This adaptation can be seen in *Sipario*, May 1947.
2. Montale, "Noia," in *Corriere della sera*, 24 Nov. 1960.
3. The standard English trans-lation "or rather to love her without complications" has been modified, since it is inaccurate.
4. *E.C.*, p. 302.

BIBLIOGRAPHY

I. MORAVIA

1. Novels and Short Stories

Gli Indifferenti, Milan (Alpes) 1929. Eng. trans., *The Time of Indifference*, tr. Angus Davidson, London (Secker & Warburg) 1953.

La bella vita, Lanciano (Carabba) 1935.

Le ambizioni sbagliate, Milan (Mondadori) 1935. Eng. trans., *The Wheel of Fortune*.

L'imbroglio, Milan (Bompiani) 1937. Eng. trans., "The Imbroglio," in *Bitter Honeymoon and Other Stories*, tr. Bernard Wall, London (Secker & Warburg) 1954; Harmondsworth (Penguin) 1961.

I sogni del pigro, Milan (Bompiani) 1940.

La mascherata, Milan (Bompiani) 1941. Eng. trans., *The Fancy Dress Party*, tr. Angus Davidson, London (Secker & Warburg) 1947.

L'amante infelice, Milan (Bompiani) 1943. Eng. trans., "The Unhappy Lover," in *B.H.* 1954.

L'epidemia, Rome (Documento) 1944.

Agostino, Milan (Bompiani) 1944. Eng. trans., *Agostino*, tr. Beryl de Zoete, London (Secker & Warburg) 1947. Reprinted in *Two Adolescents*, Harmondsworth (Penguin) 1960.

Due cortigiane, Rome (L'Acquario) 1945.

La romana, Milan (Bompiani) 1947. Eng. trans., *The Woman of Rome*, tr. Lydia Holland, London (Secker & Warburg) 1949; Harmondsworth (Penguin) 1952.

La disubbidienza, Milan (Bompiani) 1948. Eng. trans., *Disobedience*, tr. Angus Davidson, London (Secker & Warburg) 1950. Reprinted in *T.A.*, 1960.

L'amore coniugale e altri racconti, Milan (Bompiani) 1949. Eng. trans., *Conjugal Love*, tr. Angus Davidson, London (Secker & Warburg) 1950; Harmondsworth (Penguin) 1964.

Il conformista, Milan (Bompiani) 1951. Eng. trans., *The Conformist*, tr. Angus Davidson, London (Secker & Warburg) 1952.

Racconti, Milan (Bompiani) 1952. Eng. trans.: a selection from this book and from *L'amore coniugale e altri racconti* appeared in *B.H.*, and a further selection as *The Wayward Wife and Other Stories*, tr. Angus Davidson, London (Secker & Warburg) 1960; Harmondsworth (Penguin) 1963.

Racconti romani, Milan (Bompiani) 1954. Eng. trans., *Roman Tales*, tr. Angus Davidson, London (Secker & Warburg) 1956; Harmondsworth (Penguin) 1959.

Il disprezzo, Milan (Bompiani) 1954. Eng. trans., *A Ghost at Noon*, tr. Angus Davidson, London (Secker & Warburg) 1955; Harmondsworth (Penguin) 1964.

La ciociara, Milan (Bompiani) 1957. Eng. trans., *Two Women*, tr. Angus Davidson, London (Secker & Warburg) 1958; Harmondsworth (Penguin) 1961.

Teatro, Milan (Bompiani) 1958.

Nuovi racconti romani, Milan (Bompiani) 1959. Eng. trans., *More Roman Tales*, tr. Angus Davidson, London (Secker & Warburg) 1963.

La noia, Milan (Bompiani) 1960. Eng. trans., *The Empty Canvas*, tr. Angus Davidson, London (Secker & Warburg) 1961.

L'automa, Milan (Bompiani) 1963. Eng. trans., *The Fetish*, tr. Angus Davidson, London (Secker & Warburg) 1964.

2. Miscellaneous

The following list does not include Moravia's film criticism, published in *Espresso* and other newspapers, or the uncollected articles written from China, the U.S.A., Brazil, Spain, and other countries. The dramatic adaptation of *The Time of Indifference* was published in *Sipario*, May 1947. The introduction to *Nuovi argomenti*, edd. A.M. and A. Carocci, is unsigned.

" 'Gli Indifferenti' giudicato dall'autore," in *Tevere*, 6 Jan. 1933.

"Romanzo e biografia," in *Oggi*, 17 Dec. 1933.

"La moda del collettivismo," in *Oggi*, Feb. 1934.

"L'ora della pioggia," in *Almanacco dei Visacci*, Florence 1937.

"Moravia allo specchio," in *Omnibus*, 17 Jul. 1937.

La speranza, ossia cristianesimo e comunismo, Rome (Documento) 1944.

Introduction to G. Belli, *Cento sonetti*, Milan 1944.

Introduction to M. Leopardi, *Viaggio di Pulcinella*, Rome 1945.

"Arte e dolore," in *Città libera*, 26 Apr. 1945.

"Ricordo degli Indifferenti," in *Nuova Europa*, 4 Nov. 1945.

Introduction to W. Beckford, *Vathek*, ed. G. Pintor, Turin 1946.

"Estremismo e letteratura," in *Fiera letteraria*, 25 Apr. 1946.

"Destra e sinistra letteraria secondo A.M." (an interview with A. Pieroni), in *Fiera letteraria*, 13 Jun. 1946.

"Opinione sulla psicanalisi," in *Fiera letteraria*, 25 Jul. 1946.

"Scrittori allo specchio," in *Fiera letteraria*, 19 Sep. 1946.

"Assenza di maestri," in *Fiera letteraria*, 24 Oct. 1946.

"Pirandello (a dieci anni dalla morte)," in *Fiera letteraria*, 12 Dec. 1946.

"La borghesia," in *Dopo il diluvio: sommario dell' Italia contemporanea*, ed. D. Terra, Milan 1947, pp. 201-15.

"Un diluvio di lacrime," in *Fiera letteraria*, 9 Jan. 1947.

"Scultura di Leoncillo," in *Fiera letteraria*, 13 Mar. 1947.

"Dopoguerra bigotto (un artista contro i censori e i commissari)," in *Fiera letteraria*, 15 May 1947.

Answer to G. Petrocchi on "Dopoguerra bigotto...," in *Fiera letteraria*, 29 May 1947.

"Perché ho scritto *La Romana*," in *Fiera letteraria*, 3 Jul. 1947.

"Letteratura piu atrocità," in *Tempo*, 5 Feb. 1948; and in *Nazione italiana*, 12 Feb. 1948.

Interview for *Figaro Litteraire*, 20 Mar. 1948.

"Orgoglio e amore," in *Fiera letteraria*, 26 Jun. 1949.

"Ritratto di Machiavelli," 3rd paper of the Italian Cultural Association, Turin 1950.

"L'isola misteriosa," in *Mondo*, 23 Sep. 1950.

Introduction to an exhibition of R. Guttuso in Rome, 1951.

Introduction to G. de Maupassant, *Boule de suif e altri racconti*, Milan 1951.

Introduction to an exhibition of F. Gentilini in Venice, 1952.

Interview for *Fiera letteraria*, 6 Jan 1952.

"Boccaccio," in *Il trecento* in *Libera cattedra di storia della civiltà fiorentina*, Florence 1953.

Introduction to A. Sander, *Gli uomini, questi semidei*, Milan 1953.

"Il comunismo al potere e i problemi dell'arte," in *Nuovi argomenti*, I, Mar.-Apr. 1953.

Introduction to *Twenty Imaginary Views of the American Scene by Twenty Young Italian Artists*, tr. B. Johnson, Rome 1953.

"La gita in campagna" (a reduction of the short story "Andare verso il popolo"), Milan 1954.

"Note sul Comunismo e l'Occidente," in *Nuovi argomenti*, IX, Jul.-Aug. 1954.

"L'uomo come fine," in *Nuovi argomenti*, XI, Nov.-Dec. 1954, pp. 1-53.

"Pavese decadente," in *Corriere della sera*, 22 Dec. 1954.

Introduction to V. Brancati, *Paolo il caldo*, Milan 1955.

Introduction to B. Turkus and S. Feder, *Anonima assassini*, Florence 1955.

Il Provino, a one-act play staged at Milan, 22 Nov. 1955.

Introduction to Stendhal, *Passeggiate romane*, Florence 1956.

Answer to "9 domande sullo stalinismo," in *Nuovi argomenti*, XX, May-Jun. 1956.

"Note sul romanzo," in *Tempo presente*, I, 1 Apr. 1956.

Introduction to an exhibition of N. Berlinguer in Rome 1957.

Introduction to G. Carocci, *Racconti italiani*, Milan 1958.

"Il poeta dello stupore di sentirsi vivi (Ungaretti)," in *Letteratura*, VI (1958), pp. 325-6.

Un mese in U.R.S.S., Milan (Bompiani) 1958.

Introduction to E. Zolla, *I moralisti moderni*, Milan 1959.

Answer to "9 domande sul romanzo," in *Nuovi argomenti*, XXXVII-IX, May-Aug. 1959.

"Aforismi linguistici," in *Officina*, Aug.-Sep. 1959.

Interview in *L'Express*, 31 Dec. 1959.

Introduction to G. Patroni Griffi, *D'amore si muore*, Bologna 1960.

Introduction to A. Manzoni, *I promessi sposi*, Turin 1960.

Saggi italiani del 1959, edd. A.M. and Elemire Zolla, Milan (Bompiani) 1960.

Answer to "8 domande sulla critica letteraria in Italia," in *Nuovi argomenti*, XLIV-V, May-Aug. 1960.

Interview in *Avanti*, 1 Jan. 1961.

Interview in *Quaderni milanesi*, II (1961).

Un'idea dell'India, Milan (Bompiani) 1962.

L'uomo come fine e altri saggi, Milan (Bompiani) 1964.

II. OTHERS

The following list is, of necessity, very selective, although all the most extensive studies are included. Further bibliographical information may be found in the books by A. Limentani and E. Sanguineti (to both of whom I am indebted in the compilation of the list), and O. Del Buono.

ACCROCCA, E. F.: *Roma allo specchio nella narrativa Italiana da De Amicis al primo Moravia*, Rome 1958.

BERGIN, T. G.: "Italian Fiction Today," in *Yale Review*, XXXIX (1950), pp. 709-22.

———: "The Moravian Muse," in *Virginia Quarterly Review*, XXIX (1953), pp. 215-25.

Bo, C.: "Il posto di Moravia nella narrativa d'oggi," in *Fiera letteraria*, 18 Mar. 1951.

———: "La ciociara," in *Stampa*, 30 Apr. 1957.

———: "Romanzo e società nell'Italia degli ultimi dieci anni," in *Paragone*, VIII (1957), pp. 3-23.

BOCELLI, A.: "A.M. Scrittore," in *Nuova Antol.*, Jan. 1945, pp. 78-84.

———: "Moravia o l'imbroglio," in *Mondo*, 5 Nov. 1949.

———: "Racconti romani," in *Mondo*, 23 Mar. 1954.

———: "Disprezzo," in *Mondo*, 14 Dec. 1954.

———: "Nuovi racconti romani," in *Mondo*, 22 Sep. 1959.

———: "Ciociara," in *Mondo*, 4 Jul. 1957.

———: "Noia," in *Mondo*, 27 Dec. 1960.

BORGESE, G. A.: "Gli Indifferenti," in Corriere della sera, 21 Jul. 1929.

CASES, C.: Answer to "8 domande sulla cirica letteraria in Italia," in *Nuovi argomenti*, XLIV-V, May-Aug. 1960.

CECCHI, E.: "La disobbedienza," in *Europeo*, 1 Aug. 1948.

———: "Moravia premiato," in *Di giorno in giorno*, Milan 1954, pp. 333-6.

———: "Racconti romani," "Disprezzo," and "Ciociara," in *Libri nuovi e usati*, Naples 1958.

CHIAROMONTE, N.: "Moravia e il tarlo della coscienza," in *Sipario*, Mar. 1961.

CONTINI, G.: "Parere su un decennio," in *Letteratura*, Sep.-Dec. 1953.

COWLEY, M.: "Writers at Work," in *The Paris Review Interviews*, 1962, p. 201.

DEBENEDETTI, G.: "L'Imbroglio di Moravia," in *Saggi critici*, Milan 1955, pp. 213-22.

DEL BUONO, O.: *A. Moravia*, Milan 1962.

DELPECH, J.: "A la télévision avec Moravia," in *Les nouvelles littéraires*, 22 Apr. 1948.

———: "L'amore coniugale" and "Le ambizioni sbagliate," in *Les nouvelles littéraires*, 1 Sep. 1949.

DE MICHELIS, E.: *Introduzione a Moravia*, Florence 1954.

DE ROBERTIS, G.: "Racconti romani," in *Tempo*, 15 Apr. 1954.

———: "Il Disprezzo," in *Tempo*, 20 Jan. 1955.

FALCONI, C.: "I vent'anni di Moravia," in *Humanitas*, 1950, pp. 189-205.

———: "Da Gli indifferenti a St. Germain," in *Fiera letteraria*, 18 Mar. 1951.

FALLACARA, V.: In *Frontespizio*, Dec. 1935.

FALQUI, E.: *Prosatori e narratori del novecento italiano*, Turin 1950, pp. 431-41.

FERNANDEZ, D.: *Le roman italien et la crise de la conscience moderne*, Paris 1958, pp. 9-138.

FERRATA, G.: "Un modo di saturazione," in *Solaria*, VIII (Jan. 1930), pp. 61-2.

Fiera letteraria, 18 Mar. 1951. This issue is largely dedicated to Moravia.

FLORA, F.: "A.M.," in *Scrittori italiani contemporanei*, Pisa 1952, pp. 197-231.

FORTINI, F.: "Un conformista," in *Comunità*, v, 11 Jun. 1951.

FOSTER, K.: "A.M.," Blackfriars, May 1962.

GADDA, C. E.: "Agostino, by A.M.," in *Mondo*, 3 Nov. 1945. Reprinted in *I viaggi la morte*, Milan 1958.

GOLINO, C. L.: "A.M.," in *Modern Languages Journal*, XXXVI (1952), pp. 334-40.

———: "Some Aspects of Contemporary Italian Fiction," in *Modern Language Forum*, XXXVII (1952), pp. 1-20.

DATE DUE

MAR 0 8 1990
RETURNED

RETURNED

RETURNED
RETURNED
OCT 3 1 1991
NOV 3 0 1991
JAN 0 3
RETURNED